PRODUCTION and STAGING of PLAYS

Foreword by Sir Donald Wolfit

Part I: PLAY PRODUCTION

by Conrad Carter

Preface by Norman Marshall

Part II: STAGECRAFT

by A. J. Bradbury
and W. R. B. Howard

Preface by Harcourt Williams

ARCO PUBLISHING COMPANY, INC.
219 Park Avenue South, New York, N.Y. 10003

Published by Arco Publishing Company, Inc.
219 Park Avenue South, New York, N.Y. 10003

Third Printing, 1974

Library of Congress Catalog Card Number 63-10203
ISBN 0-668-01052-5

Printed in the United States of America

FOREWORD

by Sir Donald Wolfit, C.B.E.

THIS book is intended for those who have come to know the indefinable magic of the theatre. Their first experience of this may have arisen out of regular theatregoing, with memorable performances to give pleasure in recollection, or through personal work done to advance the Amateur Theatre.

This magic invariably stirs in the mind of the theatre-lover the desire for further knowledge of all the activities that contribute to the complex Art of the Theatre—acting, producing, costuming, make-up, lighting.

In schools and factories, in clubs and civic centres, interest that is created in the theatre is often followed by the determination to become a producer or a player, or to work "behind the scenes." But interest is not enough; knowledge is necessary. Some of this is, no doubt, acquired in haphazard fashion. This volume will be of practical assistance to all to whom it is designed to appeal, thus adding knowledge to interest and strengthening what is often the irresistible magnetism of the theatre.

CONTENTS

Part I: PLAY PRODUCTION

PREFACE

Play Production

by NORMAN MARSHALL

I HAVE a profound respect for the good amateur producer. He achieves a successful production in the face of difficulties unknown to his professional colleague. He has to be a teacher as well as a producer. As the author of this book points out, every amateur production is "a temporary School for Actors," while the professional producer is continually developing his own craft by learning from the skill and technique of the more experienced members of his company.

The amateur producer usually rehearses with actors already tired by their day's work, and who cannot be expected to rehearse with the intense concentration of the professional player whose livelihood in a fiercely competitive profession may depend on the success or failure of the show.

The fact that rehearsals of an amateur production are often spread over a long period, with several days between each rehearsal, adds to the producer's difficulties, as much time has to be spent in reminding the cast of what was done in a scene which may not have been rehearsed for a week or a fortnight. Often it is not possible to rehearse upon the stage until the dress rehearsal, and the stage itself may be of a size and shape which would appal the professional producer.

Yet in spite of these difficulties and many others which I have not enumerated, the standard of amateur production steadily grows better. This is largely due to the courses which are held for amateur producers, the criticism and advice of the better adjudicators at the drama festivals, the work of the county drama advisers, and the helpfulness of the books which have been written for the amateur producer. Here is another of these books, and one has a right to ask if it contains anything that has not already been said many times before, or whether it says it more clearly and incisively.

I think the particular excellence of this book is in the way the author instructs the producer how to plan each rehearsal so that he builds his production gradually and methodically, stage by stage. Amateur rehearsals are often messy and confused because the producer tries to cram far too much into every rehearsal.

There are many other matters over which I found myself enthusiastically agreeing with the author. For instance, his insistence on the proper distribution of emphasis in a sentence, so that the operative words are properly stressed. I often find amateur actors difficult to understand because in their anxiety to be audible they give equal importance to nearly every word, with the result that the sense of what they are saying is by no means clear. I agree with Mr. Carter that this is perhaps "the most common and glaring fault" of amateur acting, just as I agree with nearly everything else he has to say in this eminently clear and sensible book.

AUTHOR'S NOTE

IN writing this book I have had in mind, primarily, amateur producers who have had little specialized training in production and whose opportunities for tuition are limited.

By many contacts with producers I have been convinced that what is most frequently lacking is a realization of the necessity for a *reason* underlying every movement and a *meaning behind* every spoken phrase. In other words, everything that happens on the stage must be *significant*—and co-ordination between speech and action is *vital.*

The next important necessity is to have an "ordered plan" based on sound artistic principles, a general framework in which production may be built up. If I have, in some measure, impressed these two necessities on my readers, much of the purpose of this book will have been achieved.

I take this opportunity of gratefully acknowledging the unfailing editorial guidance of Mr. Harold Downs and his kindly co-operation throughout, and my sincere thanks also to Mr. Norman Marshall for his most valuable and encouraging Preface.

C. C.

CHAPTER I

WHY A PRODUCER?

YOU are an amateur actor. You have decided to devote yourself to "production." I wonder why?

Perhaps you feel you have a "flair" for imparting knowledge. Or, perhaps, you are sure you will be more fully satisfied artistically if your function is to mould the whole play under your direction than if it is merely to play a single part in it. Or it may be that your drama group has no expert producer, cannot afford a professional, and possibly, in any event, would prefer to be directed by one of their own members than by a "stranger."

In addition, of course, some amateur actors have "taken up" production because (whether they admit it or not) they *enjoy* a position of domination and authority. I assume you are not one of these! This last is the very worst reason for attempting to become a producer.

Now another "Why?" Why producer at all? The most important reason is the simplest. No art can be practised successfully in a state of chaos—and chaos can be most alarmingly created in "putting on a play". This is easily realized if one considers four analogies applicable to a producer. A dramatist needs an interpreter. A class of students requires a teacher. A ship must have a captain. An orchestra must have a conductor. A play producer must be all of these.

I shall return to these analogies frequently since they are invaluable in illustrating his functions, knowledge, and responsibilities.

This book is not a treatise on advanced technique; nor will it be of much interest to the arty-and-crafty "'ism'-worshipper." It is intended for the sincere workaday craftsman whose heart and mind are in the essentials of his job; who desires to be a competent and successful producer of amateur actors, who, in their turn, wish to express themselves expertly in drama and to give good value for money to their audiences.

Whether your "group" is small, in, perhaps, a village or town, or a big society, in a city or an important area, is immaterial. The principles are the same. The fundamental knowledge, the direction and control, are equally necessary in each, and for their acquisition certain qualities are essential. These are: sincerity, artistic integrity, and that special kind of humility which does nothing to deprive its possessor of authority and respect.

The producer must be, frequently, an autocrat; not because he enjoys autocracy, but because it is in some degree indispensable to success. He must, however, be a diplomat who never mingles diplomacy with insincerity. He must have sympathy—yet forbear to suffer fools gladly; he must be a teacher—yet no pedant; he must be a captain—yet no tyrant. He must be a conductor who knows his score—and his orchestra.

This sounds as if he must be a super-man, but such an approach to perfection is rare! It is, however, toward this ideal that the producer must strive, if he is to do his best work, and extract from others the most satisfying artistic achievement.

It is for you to decide how far these personal qualities are inherent in your case, or to what degree you can acquire them. They must be stressed, as they are fundamental. But my chief business is to deal with knowledge, and how to employ it in every department and aspect of the producer's function.

I assume that you have at least average imagination, or vision, and react readily (yet not *too* readily!) to emotional conceptions, ideas, and expressions. Before these can be applied to the work in hand, considerable practical knowledge is demanded.

First, you must know how to read a play, not as a layman reads a novel, but as one who visualizes every word and every action in relation to their "projection." To prevent your conception becoming unduly "theatrical," the play must have been read already from another angle—as if it were the story of real people, recounted by someone who knew them; or, as if they were people intimately known to you. These two very different approaches to the play are of equal importance. Ultimate vision should be based on conviction and sympathy, together with realization of all the possibilities of stage treatment.

Play reading needs, first, a special approach, or combination of approaches, and then—experience. Intensive playreading will not have been restricted to those plays that happen to be under consideration by your group. Your past reading habits, your inherent talent for acting and training, will be of immense value to you as a reader of plays. The ability to read a play as a producer should read it is a highly important factor in his knowledge.

He must also have a knowledge of the mechanical resources and essential stage equipment, and how to employ them. Considerable theatrical knowledge can be gained from books. Time spent "back-stage," in a professional theatre or a "Little Theatre" run by experienced amateurs, will be of immense assistance. Offer your personal help in the performance of any tasks, however menial, and much practical knowledge will be picked up. Don't get in the way. Don't ask questions at busy moments. Work hard, await opportune moments, and you will have your reward. You will discover the true meanings of strange technical terms, and learn how the various contrivances are employed. You will see, too, how certain emotional effects are secured with the aid of lighting changes, scenery, furniture, and clothing—even the speed at which the curtain is lowered at the end of an act will be instructive. In short, you will remember what you have *read*, and see it applied in practice. Do not, however, fear that you will remain ignorant if you fail to get the entrée back-stage. In co-operation with your stage staff, you can set to work to apply the results of study for yourself. In certain circumstances this may be the better way.

You must have a knowledge of acting in all its aspects.

Do good actors make good producers? *Must* a producer be an actor?

Broadly speaking (I write of amateurs) producers should have some inherent talent for acting and have had some training. With reservations, I answer, "The better the actor, the better the producer"—but the reservations are important!

Actors whose training and experience have been principally as "straight juveniles" frequently fail as producers. They are prone to become "typed," and to lack imagination. Their technique is less flexible because the difference between one "juvenile lead" and another, though existent, is not so apparent as the frequent difference between one "character" part and another. One of the vices of acting is the tendency of "juveniles" to play every part alike, ignoring the fact that every author conceives a different person in his "juvenile" from any other, while the actor is prone to stamp each of these parts too deeply with his own personality, style, and mannerisms.

The best actor-producers are "character" actors. The essence of their job is the impersonation of a very *special* character—or, rather, a series of special characters in which imagination and observation of real life play a great part. He who can change himself from one to the other with relative ease is usually an artist whose technique is, by training and experience, flexible. If he is lucky (and wise), he does not become "typed." On the professional stage even "character" actors find their range limited by unavoidable circumstances—a fate the amateur can more easily evade.

The producer must be knowledgeable about the technique of acting, and, in his capacity of teacher, be able to impart his knowledge with confidence, authority, and speed. A brief thumb-nail sketch, a momentary "impersonation," are worth far more than ten minutes' academic dissertation.

He must have a sound grasp of stage lighting—he

need not be an expert electrician, for he will have technicians at his command—but he must know what lighting effects he requires, by what equipment, colours, intensities, and lighting angles they are achieved.

He must familiarize himself with the *décor*, furniture, properties, and costume of the period of the play, also with the movement, gestures, and manners of the time. Further, he must be something of an expert in make-up, able to teach and to do it. Every amateur actor should be well-trained in make-up, self-reliant, and need only the producer's check-over. In short, the cast must learn its job in every department of theatrecraft.

Although the aim is to make amateur actors as expert as professionals (so far as their inherent aptitudes and abilities permit!), the producer of an amateur group has special problems that do not face the producer of professionals—and vice-versa.

The professional producer has at his disposal a cast, each member of which has already acquired technical knowledge and skill. True, the knowledge and skill vary, but he is rarely, if ever, faced with an untrained and completely inexperienced actor. Therefore, in a broad sense, he is not required to "teach acting." His back-stage technicians are "professional," too, and thus his entire approach is different.

The personal, or social "atmosphere" differs between the professional and the amateur company. The bread and butter of professionals depend on their work. Amateurs work for the "love" of it—not, let us hope, for the mere "fun."

The artistic aim should be similar, but the approach in many respects must be different. Rehearsal procedure is different, too. Certain "rules and regulations," however, are common to both. They are willingly obeyed by professionals without any loss of dignity. There is no excuse for amateurs who will not submit to the same general principles of discipline, since they are vital to artistic success. It is for the producer to know what these are, their purpose, and to enforce them with understanding and tact, yet implacably.

CHAPTER II

THE PRODUCER AND HIS AUTHOR

THE producer is the interpreter of the author to the actor; therefore, it is manifest that he must "speak the author's language"—in other words, thoroughly understand the play and the author's intention.

The "dual approach" in reading a play, namely, the "real people" angle and the "stage presentation" conception has already been discussed. The producer's personal study of the play should be in this order, forgetting, first of all, about the theatre and that he is going to produce the play. It is even preferable, at this stage, if casting has not taken place, so that visualization shall not be coloured by pre-conceived ideas.

The play must be read with understanding and sympathy. If the producer finds himself quarrelling with the author, the passage must be read again and again; if he is still at variance, judgment must be suspended until the whole play has been read a second time. There are many dramatists, both celebrated and relatively unknown, the true qualities of whose work cannot be appraised fully, even by expert readers, at the first or even the fourth reading. Their plays "grow on" the reader rather than create an immediate, vivid impression. As an editor and "play doctor," I have read many such, and among what are now my favourite plays are a great number that, on first reading, awakened in me but little enthusiasm.

Conversely, I would say to the novice, "Beware lest an instant response to 'brilliance' leads you astray. Every play demands sober reflection before a final verdict is given."

While reading, the producer must absorb himself in the atmosphere not only of the period but also of the house, its inhabitants, the "emotional colour" of the play, its "shape," and its purport. He must ask himself innumerable questions about "what the author is driving at" and strive to give himself sound, convincing answers. Then, to employ the "orchestra" analogy, the producer must decide the "key" in which the play is written and the "over-all character" of the composition. Matters such as *tempo*, climax, and so on present themselves with the "stage" approach. Not yet will the producer have concerned himself very much with individual characters other than, perhaps, the leading protagonists—at least, not consciously.

Now on fairly intimate terms with his absent author, the producer relaxes mentally and allows the play to "take hold" of him. During this process he will invariably find unexpected light breaking in on some darkened places.

Next the play is studied from the "theatre angle." As he reads, the producer, more or less consciously, visualizes the play *in production*—he even "hears" the characters speaking and "sees" them in action. (This is still before casting). Obscurities diminish, but he need not worry greatly if a few remain.

The play now presents itself as a piece of dramatic literature, an example (irrespective of faults) of stagecraft, seen in perspective and awaiting the interpretive mind. Some written notes should be made, for the time is approaching when the producer must prepare his script—a process dealt with in Chapter III. First, however, he must be quite decided about all the major (and some of the minor) elements of interpretation, and matters of balance between scene and scene, between character and character. Problems will arise, both mechanical and personal. For the moment, the latter are the more important, for the play must now be cast. In all this, complete sincerity, artistic integrity, and inflexible fidelity to your author, so far as you have understood him, are essential.

Contrary to the apparent belief of some of our ultra-modern producers, it is neither their nor their actors' business to "re-write," in a production or an acting sense, any author's play. Capable dramatists who write with their tongues in their cheeks are, on the whole, rare. The majority are skilled writers, and many have a sound working knowledge of stagecraft. Both producer and actor may succeed in enriching a playwright's work, but they are only creative artists in the sense that they transmute the written word into human action and speech and set them in an acceptable visible frame that contributes to the author's purpose.

It *is* the producer's business to be correct in his estimation of "key" and "characterization" because these will, above all, influence his "treatment," both mechanical and emotional. This does not mean that some genuine misconceptions must of necessity destroy the play, provided they are not fundamental.

It is not, however, helpful to play a straight comedy as a somewhat artificial comedy of manners or a satire; or a "light comedy" as an extravagant farce, or naturalistic drama as if it were the latest thing in experimental "expressionism." The precise touch of farcical extravagance, of artificiality, or of imaginative fantasy must be estimated as nearly as possible. It is sometimes, but not always, the author's fault that the producer blunders. The fundamentals having been decided, that very important duty to the author must be faced—

Casting

The position of the producer on the casting committee can be, and frequently is, difficult. Some producers (the cowards!) refuse to serve on it, and reserve their complaints until later. How foolish to court disaster in this way! He knows what he needs, and the best possible casting is half-way towards getting it. Moreover, in the amateur theatre there is far more embarrassment caused by re-casting when rehearsals have started than by refusal to agree on certain castings while in committee. The captain of the ship must share in the responsibility of engaging the crew!

The best method, undoubtedly, is by audition before a small committee of which the producer is a member. The auditions should be followed by a general play-reading of the provisional cast, before final decisions are made. I have always found it most valuable to impress on the cast that they are still provisional until the first few rehearsals have taken place. This avoids some of the "hard feelings" should it prove that the committee have erred in judgment.

At the auditions, each candidate should be interviewed in camera. The committee is dealing with amateurs who frequently cannot do themselves justice in the presence of even friendly rivals! The "I-know-I-shall-be-dreadful-if-that-Jones-woman-is-in-the-room" state of mind is often excusable. In any event, privacy is the fairest method. The best way of getting a true estimate of an actor's suitability is to treat him on this occasion with sympathy, understanding, and encouragement—while tactfully checking any tendency to over-confidence.

Each candidate should have had a copy of the play and ample time to study it. Intelligent sight-reading is not a common accomplishment. I have been present at many "readings" where expensively educated people have been sadly incapable of expressive reading and have displayed barely a nodding acquaintance with vocal punctuation—an argument in favour of more and more play readings!

In any event, both amateurs and professionals are usually at their worst during an audition. If you and/or the committee "see" the candidate in the part but his audition is disappointing, discuss the character briefly with him and allow him to re-read the scene, or some other passage in which he may do himself more justice. Conversely, you will be surprised at times how an actor whom it has not occurred to you would be ideal in a certain character will show up well at an audition. You must not set too much store on this, but it does call for serious comparison with the favourite you have, perhaps, already backed.

There is one inflexible attitude the producer must adopt in casting; he must not be moved by any personal or private matters. Neither social standing, private relationship, ticket-selling capacity, nor any other non-artistic factor must ever concern him. The suitability of an artist in a given part is the producer's sole consideration. The ultimate responsibility is his, and the committee must provide the human material nearest to his ideal. In the amateur theatre, occasional limited compromise is inevitable. At the same time, the producer, though he will get the credit if proved right, must also be prepared to take the rap if proved wrong. But he cannot be expected to bear full responsibility if his artistic convictions are over-ruled.

Physical Appearance or Acting Ability?

Manifestly, the ideal is the actor who "looks the part" and who also has the right conception and acting ability. But, in an amateur production, there is rarely an unlimited choice.

The author sees HUBERT as "a tall, fair young man of military bearing, with a firm chin and keen blue eyes." You can hardly give that part to George, who is forty, under medium height, "a little thin on top," and displays the early signs of "middle-aged spread." Decision must be made on how much of the description is essential to the play. Probably "young" and "military bearing" are the two vital factors, but with these must be considered the appearance of the actor or actress most associated with him. Apart from these, intelligent interpretation is everything.

JULIE is "a pretty little thing, with dark brown curls, sympathetic eyes, and a ready, kindly smile that lights up her face with eagerness and vivacity." Obviously, the actress must not be very tall and gaunt, nor exceptionally buxom. It will not matter if she is blonde. If, however, she has a "hard" face, she will possibly possess too cold a nature and a "hard" attitude to life. Will she understand and sympathize with JULIE? Will she, irrespective of her technical skill, succeed in projecting the author's conception? These two questions demand decisive answers. One may feel in this instance that JULIE'S *nature* is far more important than her *appearance*, although some approximation to the latter will assist the audience in "seeing" the character through the author's eyes. In this department of casting, compromise is more possible than in any other.

"Conception" or "Skill"?

The producer must, after compromise on "physical appearance," weigh the relative values of "imaginative conception" as against "technical skill." These two qualities do not always march together! I have, on countless occasions, been faced with an actor or actress of considerable training and experience yet lamentably lacking in ability to visualize the character or conceive the nature and degree of the emotions through which he or she must pass during the traffic of the play. Tough experience has shown me that in the majority of such cases I would far rather teach everything technical to a novice who has "conception" (and enthusiasm) than rehearse a skilled artist to whom the character is a completely intellectual and spiritual stranger. The work may be harder in one sense but invariably more rewarding!

"Personality Value" and "Balance"

Acting is a mutual, or *reciprocal*, function. We do not (or should not!) act in hermetically-sealed compartments. It follows, therefore, that in casting, considerable attention must be paid to this. The point is not only "Is Gerald the ideal SIR HENRY?" but also "Is

Gerald the ideal SIR HENRY *when playing opposite Edna as* HARRIET?"—and vice versa. Men and women all have their own "weight" of personality, both as individuals and as artists. The producer must gauge the precise degree of domination of one character over another so that balance is not destroyed. In the same way, he will judge how far *in individual scenes* one character dominates at one time and another at another. This is quite distinct from how the various scenes are played so that "story balance" is preserved.

Personality value and balance are bound up with considerations of appearance and physique that cannot be ignored. Normally, a hen-pecked husband will be visualized as much smaller than the domineering wife. Heavy personality is popularly associated with heavy physique! Yet it may well be that the author's fun derives largely from a tiny woman "crushing" a great lumbering spouse!

How true it is that the conductor must know his composer, his score—and his orchestra, too.

CHAPTER III

THE PRODUCER AND HIS SCRIPT

YOU have studied your play, and you understand it. You have cast it as satisfactorily as possible. There is, however, much to do before the first "reading rehearsal" is held.

Probably, you have an "acting edition" of the play, i.e., the play with "stage directions" introduced at appropriate places, a ground plan, perhaps an illustration of the original "settings," a list of the required furniture and properties, and even a "lighting plot." On the other hand, you may have a copy of the play with only the slightest indications of setting and action. You may even possess little more than a typescript of the dialogue.

However sparsely or fully your "script" is annotated, it will require careful preparation.

"Acting Editions"

Are "acting editions" good or bad? Every producer must be his own judge. There are acting editions—and acting editions! Some are detailed, accurate, and invaluable to the tyro-producer. Some are "fairly competent," and others are disastrous in their inaccuracy and ambiguity. Only experience will teach you how far any edition is dependable. Let us leave it at that.

So far as the setting is concerned, you must take advantage of any information in the edition that is appropriate to the theatre, or hall, and the stage at your disposal. A great deal of what must be rejected for material reasons can, however, suggest possible improvisations. You will not be expected (it would be foolish to make the attempt) to reproduce on the stage of a parish hall (proscenium opening 20 ft., with a working depth of 14 ft.) everything in a photograph of the setting at the Hellinger Theatre, New York. Moreover, it is unnecessary to do so if you can faithfully suggest the setting, or the vital parts of it, and convey the general character and atmosphere of the play. The producer's business is to decide what is vital and what is not.

Again, the structure of the theatre and its stage may make it impossible to have the entrances exactly as in the original. For instance, the back wall of the "set" may be too near the permanent wall of the stage to permit a door in the back wall of the "room." It will, therefore, have to be up-stage in the R or L wall, and it may be helpful if this doorway is set in a short piece of angled wall. This provides for more effective entrances and exits by the characters, and off-stage space to show the "backing" beyond the door. Similar considerations may apply to other doors and windows. A producer must be able to improvise and to adapt to all working conditions.

Some furniture will be omitted, and much of it will be of a reduced size. Care should be exercised to retain the character of the pieces, even if their proportions must be varied.

The Ground Plan

This must be drawn to scale. It should be large, for the benefit of the stage staff. A large plan ready to hand makes easier the "marking up" of the script. Smaller replicas can be drawn later, one to slip into your own copy of the play and another into that of your stage manager, who will be an ever-present shadow at rehearsals. The scale should be at least $\frac{1}{2}$ in. to the foot. If the stage is small, the scale can be larger, say $\frac{3}{4}$ in. to the foot.

In constructing the ground plan, the first consideration must be the problem of "the lines of sight." It is useless to plan a setting and then to discover that members of the audience in the side seats cannot see some of the important action. Remember, too, that it is within the precise limits of the stage setting that the company must always rehearse.

In the theatre or hall will be taken the precise measurements of the stage, the "proscenium opening"—i.e., the width between the uprights of the proscenium arch, allowing for the possible intrusion of the curtain ("house tabs"), which cannot always be drawn back out of sight. The depth from the "setting line" (an imaginary line across the stage between the down-stage edges of the scenery on either side) to the back wall of the stage should also be estimated. This measurement does not represent the full "working depth," for allowance must be made for space in which the characters may cross the stage behind the scenery, or the distance necessary between a stage window and the back-cloth or backing depicting the distance scene, or any essential space required for a door in the back wall of the "set," beyond which there will be a piece of "interior backing" to represent the "other room," a corridor, or a porch.

Next should be ascertained, by tactful and careful

inquiry, just where the front row of seats will be placed; how far the row will be from the edge of the proscenium arch, precisely where the extreme-end seats or chairs will be set, and the width of the side aisles. If there is a balcony at the back of the hall, it will be useful to know its height and distance, and also the height of the proscenium above stage level. In some productions, certain action could be obscured from the audience in the back of the balcony, but this question does not arise if the proscenium is reasonably high in relation to the balcony.

From these data should be drawn a plan similar to the illustration (Fig. 1). This shows a hall where the "line of sight" is a comparatively simple problem.

Note that the thin double lines represent the permanent walls. The heavy lines show the "scenery flats." The "broken" lines, drawn from the centres of the extreme seats, Row A. Nos. 1 and 16, to the corners of the proscenium arch and thence to the back of the scene, show the limits of vision for the occupants of these seats. They will be the greatest, but not the only, sufferers.

It is clear that a character "A," standing on the hearth-rug L with his back to the fire will be just seen. A character "B" entering R, will be seen an instant later, and almost to the last moment of his exit. Almost the entire setting will be within the visual range of every member of the audience with the exception of those who occupy A1 and A16, who, however, will only suffer the loss of what is contained between the lines of sight and the side flats, in which slender areas no important action that MUST be seen by all should be allowed to take place.

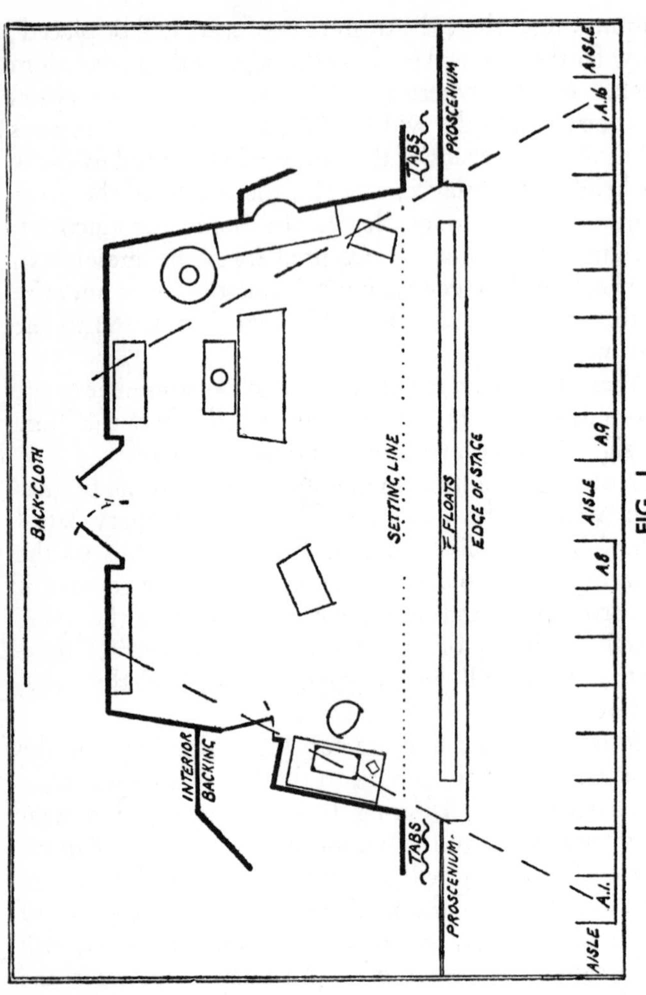
BACK-CLOTH
INTERIOR BACKING
TABS
PROSCENIUM
TABS
PROSCENIUM
SETTING LINE
FLOATS
EDGE OF STAGE
AISLE
A.16
A.9
AISLE
A.8
A.1.
AISLE

FIG. 1

In Fig. 1, the door R has been set "in-stage" a little by a "return," probably about 18 ins. deep, and both side-walls are set at a slight angle. It might be suggested that the walls could have been set at right angles with the "floats" and that the door R could have been down-stage, below the desk. True, but there are some reasons against this course. Adoption of this suggestion could result in an appreciable proportion of the audience losing important features of the side-walls, and the characters playing with their backs to the fire would be excessively "profiled." Moreover, down-stage is a bad place for a leading character to make an important entrance. Players enter thus at a "non-dominant" spot, and almost immediately have to travel in a somewhat UP-stage direction. This nearly always robs such an entrance of some effectiveness.

Imagine a situation in which the setting is as in Fig. 1.

The only occupant of the stage is SIR HENRY, a cold, unemotional man, who is seated at the desk, R, writing. HARRIET, who is a little afraid of him, enters R. She is almost immediately visible, and registers a reaction on finding him there:

HARRIET (*reacting*). Oh—there you are, Henry.
SIR HENRY (*without turning; coldly*). Yes.
(HARRIET *closes the door quietly.*)
(*Writing.*) I wish to speak to you.
HARRIET (*reacting; in a low voice*). Oh. (*She moves slowly towards the settee.*)

Note that (*a*) SIR HENRY can be far more "crushing" by not looking up or turning to her; (*b*) HARRIET faces the house to get her reactions "over"; (*c*) no major movement is required until this "moment" has been fully registered and the "atmosphere" established.

In the setting Fig. 2, however, HARRIET, on entrance, has to react and say her line turned slightly UP-stage, and SIR HENRY's "Yes" must be said while they are, in

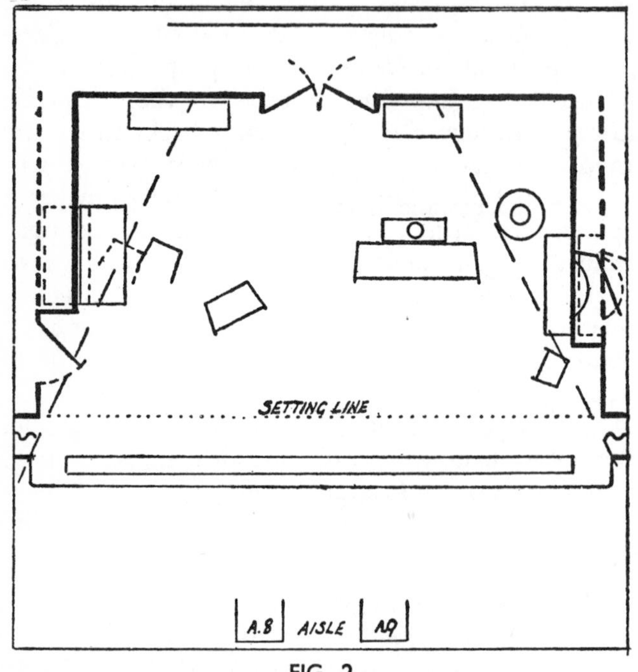

FIG. 2

a sense, facing each other, even if he does not look *up*. Then HARRIET has to "break the moment" by crossing towards C, until SIR HENRY can give his second phrase with his back to her, by which time he will not be so intensely "crushing" as he would have been with Fig. 1. Certainly the majority of entrances under Fig. 2. will lose throughout the play, since the door is DOWN-stage. The above incident would be even worse if the R wall were not set IN-stage (as the dotted lines show) and the effect of not IN-staging the L wall is also manifest. If the stage is, on the other hand, small, this in-staging causes great restriction of movement.

Drawing in the Setting

This is constructed with the setting line as a base. Walls, window, fire, and door having been drawn, fill in the furniture—as much of the original as can be accommodated and is vital. This also must be drawn to scale as nearly as possible, at first lightly in pencil, because as the script is worked through it may be necessary to adjust the positions of the pieces in order to get effective groupings on a smaller stage, and sufficient space for crossings and other movements by the characters. During this process much will be done by "trial and error," but eventually the best setting to cover all the important "pictures" and moves that the play demands will be decided.

Marking Positions, Movements, and Groups

A clear idea of positions, broad movements, and the more important dramatic groupings should be formed before entering the rehearsal room. Adjustments must be left to early rehearsals, and decisions on minor details must not be too rigid until then. Nothing convinces a cast of a producer's incompetence more than when he has to work out major movements (with inevitable changes of mind in the process!) during rehearsal.

Fig. 3 indicates the "acting areas" of a stage. The

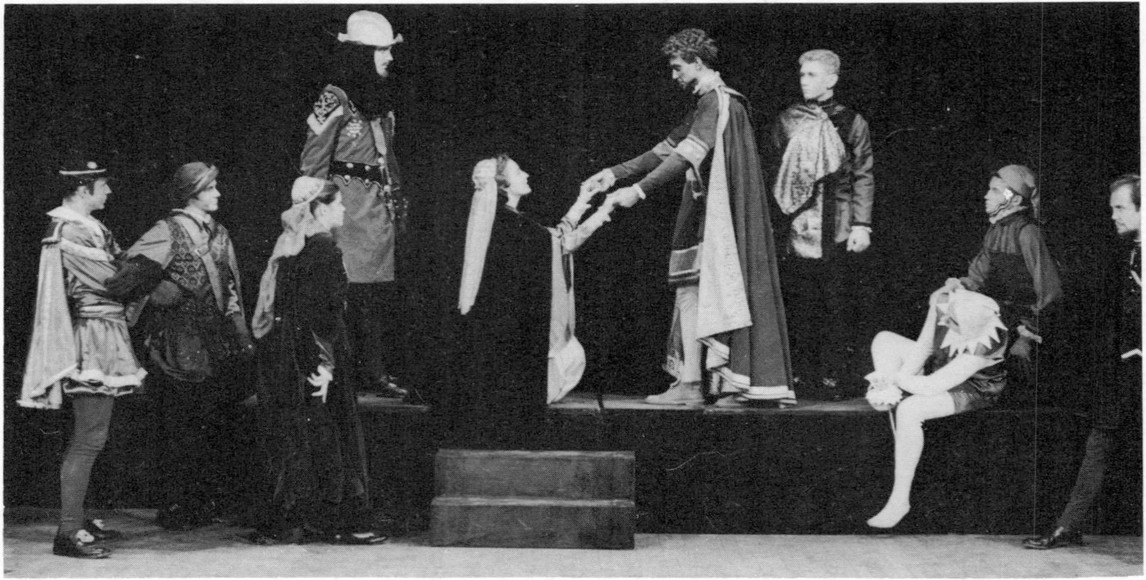

Shakespeare's "Othello" in a production by the Iowa State College Theatre. Characters are, left to right, Montano, Roderigo, Desdemona, Othello, Page, Clown, Sailor, Iago.

Courtesy ANTA

The Herald Scene in the Catholic University's production of "Othello." It was staged with elaborate sets at the University Theatre in 1951.

Courtesy ANTA

divisions drawn are arbitrary; for example, an actor may be regarded as "at RC" although he is no more than on the R edge of the C division. Again, an actor may be said to "move down to L C" without necessarily occupying the square thus designated. In this instance, the expression would mean that the player had to move DOWN-stage from an UP-stage position and

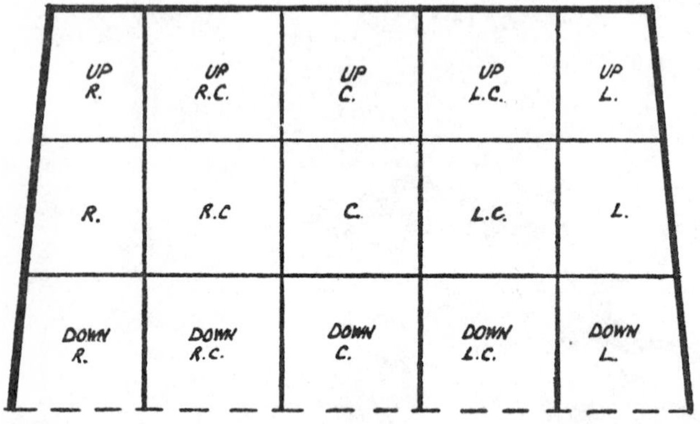

FIG. 3

was then "left of centre" without having reached the extreme L zone.

Great imagination should be exercised and cultivated during the process of "marking up," for every moment of the play. You will find it rather like a game of chess; constantly having to think one or even several moves ahead. For instance, you will have designed what appears to be a most effective "picture"—only to find, a page or so later, that you have not allowed for a quick, clean, even breath-taking exit for EDNA, some essential business for GEORGE, or a shattering entrance for HUBERT—none of which will be possible with the grouping you have devised. For instance, in Fig. 4, EDNA and JOHN are in violent conflict. They have a relatively UP-stage position, and the witnesses to this altercation are suitably grouped. But—the incident terminates with a whirlwind exit of EDNA *down L*, She has a large armchair at C, and a closely-knit trio

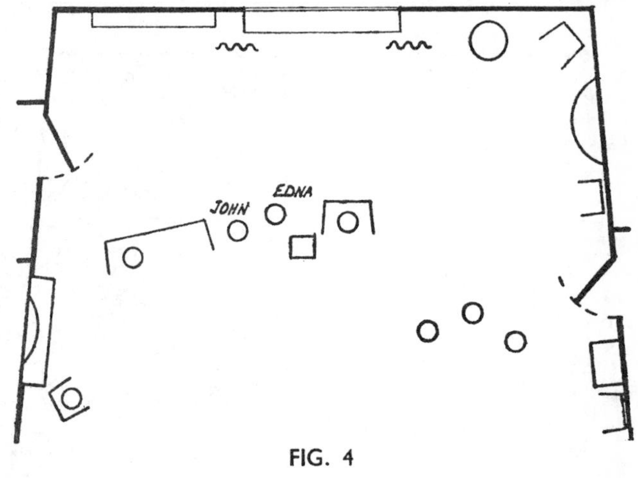

FIG. 4

down LC, barring her way. An instantaneous break-up of this trio is unthinkable, and the play demands that the picture is "held" until after her exit.

Fig. 5 shows the correct grouping. You will have to retrace your steps and now arrange that the "trio" is at R, and EDNA and JOHN are at LC. It will probably be permissible for JOHN to "ease up" level with EDNA just before her exit-cross, or she may be able to brush him aside (a little up and to L) to give herself a clean cross. She will, by the way, probably divide her last line, using the final phrase as an "exit line" as she goes out. There is, however, no hard and fast rule for this. Everything depends on the character, the line, and the purport of the scene. This principle is applied to every instance of "manœuvring" characters. If GEORGE must quickly and most unexpectedly produce a document or revolver from a bureau, he must be cunningly manœuvred into position in time, neither too early nor

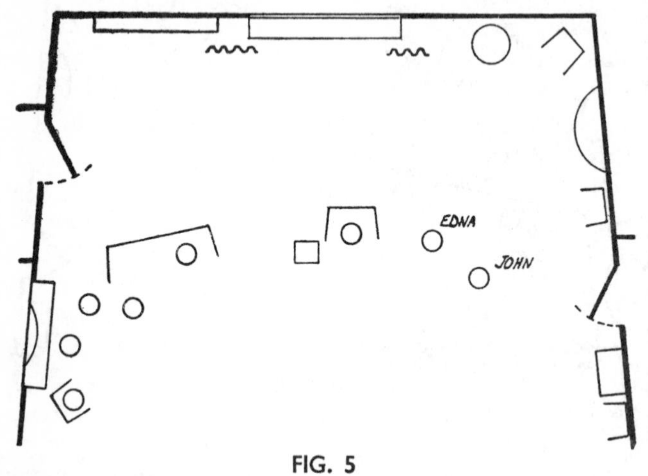

FIG. 5

unconvincingly "just in time"! You will find it an intricate business that demands imagination, thought, and patience. Yet how fascinating it proves to be!

Whether you are a beginner or not, do not despise the stage directions supplied. If the entrances and the arrangement of the furniture do not vary drastically from the original, these directions will be helpful. Ask yourself constantly WHY they have been so devised; you will invariably find that although they appear to concern the mechanics of acting they are also of great emotional significance. For instance, "dramatic domination" is influenced largely by position on the stage. Broadly, a character cannot dominate another, or a group, from a DOWN-stage position. If he is downstage near C he has nothing to address but the floats! If down R or down L, he must "play up-stage" or partly profiled, which, again, robs him of domination, unless, perhaps, he is perched on a rostrum, a low staircase, or on some structure that raises him above stage level. Even then, this position is rarely of maximum effectiveness. Styles of acting and production vary with the character of the play, but this fundamental truth remains, that the most dominant position for any character at any moment is UP C, or UP-stage near C, with the subordinate characters DOWN-stage in relation to himself. The tyrannical father, the commanding officer, the dictator, the criminal with the revolver, the revengeful woman facing her victims—for all of these, *that* must be the relative position when the moment of domination or threat is reached. While marking the script in preparation, these broad principles must be applied.

Stage Directions

Stage directions are of two kinds. There are the "mechanical" directions that concern those things just discussed, and there are those that may be regarded purely as "emotional" directions. These concern "how a line is spoken" and details of action and reaction to portray feeling. They are often valuable indications of the effect the author wishes to convey, but they must not be accepted as dogmatic instructions on the means to be employed. We act from the inside, outwards; our portrayal is through the medium of the actor's personality—harnessed to his craftsmanship. The actor visualizes the part in the light of his conception of the author's intention, but "A" will project that idea (or attempt to do so) by a somewhat different method from that employed by "B." "A," in co-operation with his producer, will decide that a line is more—or less—intense, or satirical, or tender than "B" and *his* producer, and so on. This is more fully discussed in Chapters V and VI.

Many of these "emotional stage directions" are legitimate, and cannot be ignored. Such suggestions as "gently," "coldly," "ironically," and "gaily," are quite in order and—all too frequently!—necessary. Even "looking down shyly" and "clenching his fists" are hints that can be accepted in many cases. When, however, an author goes into detail and insists on a character "snarling through his teeth," "tearing his hair and waving his arms wildly," and other shades of facial expression and gesture, I think the actor is justified in asking himself whether he is to *act* or turn himself into a marionette! Mr. "X" will register admirably by doing just what the author says (in moderation!) while Mr. "Y" will, on the other hand, give a superb performance by doing nothing of the kind.

Since, however, as a producer of amateurs, you will have to give instruction in the craft of acting, your own ideas should be noted on your script but left fairly "open" until you see of what the actors are capable imaginatively and in projection.

Points on "suspense," "climax," "pause," and changes of *tempo* should also be included tentatively. A few small but accurate sketches—ground plans in miniature—should be made, and inserted in your copy at the appropriate pages in order to show what the grouping is to be at given points in the play. Do not regard the script as "marked" until everything has been considered a second, or even a third, time.

CHAPTER IV

THE PRODUCER AND HIS STAFF

THE captain of the ship performs his duties chiefly on the bridge and in the chart room. He makes no attempt to stoke, lubricate, or control the engines, to cook the meals in the galley, to dispatch radio messages, or to organize deck sports. His responsibility is to see that the ship reaches the correct port, safely and on time.

The play producer, similarly, does not make the scenery, obtain furniture, lights and props, control the switchboard, raise and lower the "tabs," or sell programmes.

The essence of good organization is not doing things but getting things done—by other people. There is a good deal of truth in this saying.

On the other hand, neither the post of producer nor of captain is a sinecure. Yet both are dependent for success on an adequate, competent, and loyal staff.

Although some reduction may be made safely if the show is not "heavy" as to scenery or complicated in other respects, the full personnel for the producer of an amateur company is:

STAGE DIRECTOR
STAGE MANAGER
ASSISTANT STAGE MANAGERS (1 or 2)
ELECTRICIAN
ASSISTANT ELECTRICIAN
PROPERTY MASTER
WARDROBE MISTRESS

In addition there are such stage hands as the production requires for scene-shifting and similar duties.

The functions of each member of the staff may be described thus:

The STAGE DIRECTOR is, in effect, the deputy-producer, who will always take rehearsals should the producer be unavoidably absent. He will usually rehearse understudies. He is the closest associate of the producer, and acts as liaison officer between him and the rest of the staff. If the company is small and the production relatively simple (particularly if the theatre is not large), his office can be merged into that of the—

STAGE MANAGER, the S.M., in whom is vested considerable authority. He confers with and receives from the producer and stage director the schedules ("plots") of all the material and mechanical requirements for the production. These are: scenery; furniture; properties; sound and other "effects."

The lighting plot is not included in these, for this goes (perhaps via the stage director) direct from the producer to the electrician.

The S.M. and his assistants (under the S.D. if such an official is appointed) are responsible for receiving hired scenery and its "setting up."

If the company makes and paints its own scenery, the S.M. has the similar duties of ensuring that it is right in dimensions, design and *décor*.

The stage director and/or the S.M., are directly responsible to the producer for securing by hire or loan all the furniture, hangings, pictures, and stage props. These are submitted to the producer for approval before final arrangements are made.

The stage director and/or the S.M. are provided

with marked copies of the play. He, or one of his assistants, must be present at and watch *every* rehearsal. Any revisions or adjustments of positions, movements, or "business" made in rehearsal are inserted in the copy at the time. This saves argument on future occasions, and thus a "prompt copy" is prepared as rehearsals proceed.

During the rehearsal period, the S.M. must bring to the notice of the stage director or the producer any problems arising out of the provision of the items set out in the "plots," for nothing must be left until the eleventh hour. Periodic conferences to report progress are advisable.

At all stage and dress rehearsals, and at all performances, the S.D. or the S.M. has full control of the stage area and everything that happens in his department. He also has considerable authority over the players. If their presence "on stage" (whether the curtain be up or down) interferes with smooth working, he can dismiss them to their dressing-rooms. He will also enforce the NO TALKING and NO SMOKING orders, both of which should have been made crystal-clear to the cast beforehand.

The stage director and/or the stage manager with their staff set the stage and furniture before each act. The producer is not expected to be present, having duties elsewhere (See Chapter X) until the stage is ready to be "passed."

ASSISTANT STAGE MANAGER. For a three-act production, two "A.S.M's" are advisable. Their duties are primarily concerned with those of the S.M., whose subordinates they are. When the ordinary stage hands have set the scenery, with or without the assistance of the S.M. and the A.S.M's, the latter help to set and to adjust the furniture, hangings, etc. The A.S.M's will also be responsible for "stage props" such as crockery, cutlery, and food for meals, the revolver in the desk, the telegram on the mantel-shelf, and the incriminating document in the Chinese vase! It is not unusual, if these duties do not prove too onerous, to add to them by making one A.S.M. the prompter and the other the call-boy. The former should have attended several rehearsals and, indeed, officiated as "prompt" thereat in order that he or she may be familiar with the text and know where "pauses" occur and the duration of each. The call-boy A.S.M. will rehearse himself at the final rehearsals. His function is to knock at all dressing-room doors and to call "Half-hour, please." This is repeated for "Quarter of an hour" and also "Beginners, please," five minutes before the beginning of the overture music. The call-boy should also call all players during performance some minutes before they are due to make each entrance, unless they have observed that the player is already waiting in the wings. The call-boy (or one of the A.S.M's) should also be made responsible for checking "personal" or "hand" props with each player. For this purpose the A.S.M. is supplied with a "Personal Property Plot." A section of it will read something like this:

ACT I.

SIR HENRY Cigarette case, filled. Lighter.
(*2nd entrance.*) Telegram.
(*3rd entrance.*) Broken porcelain statuette.

HARRIET Handbag containing compact, handkerchief, and diary. Pencil.

(*2nd entrance.*) Letter—blue paper—opened. No handbag.
(*4th entrance.*) Small green bottle. Bandage on "cut" finger.

Many amateur players are just as reliable over personal props as any professional; the ultimate responsibility must be theirs. It does no harm, however, to have a check, especially in an exceptionally exciting and complicated play, or one with frequent exits and re-entrances.

The PROPERTY MASTER is one whose duties are sometimes merged into that of the S.M., who not infrequently has a gift for making unusual "props." Parchment documents impressively sealed, Renaissance goblets, blood-stained daggers, spinning-wheels, and Chinese idols joyfully occupy his long winter evenings, and who can produce the ancestral portrait more mysteriously, yet convincingly, than he? Sometimes he manifests himself as the *alter ego* of the stage carpenter. Sometimes, alas, he does not exist at all, and his miracles must be the product of communal effort.

The WARDROBE MISTRESS and her own staff function only when a "costume play" is in hand. She confers directly with the producer, and together they bring out a costume plot, in which style, colour, and other details are included. The wardrobe mistress superintends the measurement-taking of each actor or actress, including wig measurements, and fills up the charts usually supplied by the theatrical costumiers for this purpose. When the "wardrobe" is received, the wardrobe mistress and assistants unpack, check, and hand out the costumes. These are tried on and paraded, after which the wardrobe staff are responsible for the return and exchange of costumes that are wrong, for minor alterations, and for repairs during the run of the play. Finally, they are responsible for the return of the costumes in good order to the hiring firm.

The Stage Electrician usually works directly with the producer during the preparatory stages, the S.D. co-operating. The electrician is a technician in electrical matters, and by experience becomes a useful adviser on how various effects and "atmospheres" are secured in terms of light. On the other hand, although the producer may not know an "ohm" from an "amp" or a "watt" from a "volt," he must acquire a working knowledge of stage lighting equipment, types of lamps, and the purpose of each; colour media, how to mix and control these; the intensities and angles of direction of light beams for the achievement of the desired results.

The initial co-operation with the producer must be a discussion of how far the available lighting equipment will provide for the lighting cues in the plot, and to what extent additional equipment should be hired, if this is permissible. The electrician may be in a position to suggest methods whereby reasonable results may be obtained with the existing installation. Since this is not a textbook on stage lighting, technical details are not discussed here. They are dealt with specially in another volume in this Series. It should be stressed, however, that the lighting plot should be clearly expressed; also that the stage electrician is master on the switchboard, as the S.D. or S.M. is on the stage.

The wise producer will call a conference, or series of

conferences, with all his staff, before rehearsals begin. When all are fully briefed, he should leave them to their individual jobs (except for progress reports), for now he is to meet his cast, formally and in force, for the first time.

CHAPTER V

THE PRODUCER AND HIS CAST

THERE is no form of activity in which cordial personal relationships, mutual understanding, and a "happy atmosphere" are more necessary than in play production. The creation and maintenance of these depend greatly, though not wholly, on the producer. He need not possess all the virtues and nobilities of character, and no human failings. At the same time, he must steer successfully between the Scylla of dictatorship and the Charybdis of excessive "easy good-fellowship."

It is wise to make it clear from the first that, without any ill-feeling, there must be no "nonsense." At the same time, the producer must never allow any member of cast (or staff) to feel afraid to approach him, nor must he ever withhold genuine sympathy and advice.

He will soon find, on the other hand, that there are a few types (not confined only to the amateur stage) of which he must beware, and with which he must be firm from the beginning. Here are some examples, none of them imagined. All have been encountered by every producer:

(1) The actor (and actress) who delivers himself (or herself) thus: "Of course, Mr. X, you understand that I never even begin to give a performance until the last week of rehearsal—I *mean*, I never give a *thing* until then." Fantastic? No—surprisingly common. These

precious creatures really believe that this attitude is a proof of genius. They choose to forget—or are unaware—that our great actors have, substantially, the opposite approach. Where would a company be, I wonder, if they did not know until the last few days how Mr. Alec Guinness and Miss Edith Evans proposed to play their parts? As the character "grows on" the player it begins to flower, and his fellow players, observing the growth, develop their own portrayals in harmony, even if there be conflict and adjustment *en route*. This is what is meant by true reciprocal acting. Let there be no mistake; this kind of player must change his or her attitude at once, or the part must be re-cast immediately.

(2) The player who will *not* "take production." He or she will soon be known. It will be obvious tacit rebellion, not inability. The danger here is twofold. First, this subtle form of mutiny spreads infection. Moreover, if it is not dealt with, you are faced with a worse danger, namely, that the player will, eventually, yield, play as required in rehearsal, and then deliberately betray you and the members of the cast by reverting to his or her own rendering when the curtain has risen on the public performance. Such a thing sounds as incredible as my first example, but I have met this individual too often to have any illusions on the subject. This type of player demands firm, nay, relentless treatment. There must be an early understanding and an honourable pledge. If ultimate treachery follows, the player must never be permitted to play for that company again.

Then we have the cheerful "I'll be all right on the night-er," the unpunctual, the habitual absentee, the player who wants to debate with you on every conceivable point, and, perhaps, variants of these. But perhaps I have given you sufficient advice on (1) and (2) to cover most of your personal problems!

Acting Abilities

The producer must try to gauge the degree of acting skill of each of his players as soon as he can. This will assist him in estimating which scenes will need most tuition in technique. Occasionally, he will find that a novice will require less intensive rehearsal than experienced artistes because the conception of the former happens to be more vivid than that of the latter. It is not uncommon to find, moreover, that the beginner adheres more faithfully to correct technique than do some "old hands," who, in the course of time, have slipped into bad acting-habits. Perhaps I should apologize for the cliché, but there is such a thing as the familiarity that breeds contempt!

Conferences and Readings

Before the first rehearsal, the producer will be well advised to hold at least one "round-table conference" with his cast, followed by a "reading" and one or two subsequent readings.

The conference must be frank, and even the humblest participant encouraged to express views and ideas. It is necessary for the players to learn what is the producer's interpretation of the author's intention. It is no less vital for the producer to discover what, up to this time, have been the reactions of every member of the cast to the study of the play. The resultant discussions should establish in the minds of all the "key" of the composition, and also clear ideas of individual characterization.

Having achieved a reasonable measure of agreement, the members of the cast proceed to a reading of the play, being first enjoined to keep in mind, as they read, the fundamentals on which they are in accord.

During the first reading, the producer should try not to interrupt. He must listen intently and make written notes. The reading over, he deals with the points noted, stresses misconceptions, and reminds the cast of forgotten matters. Now the cast reads the play again, endeavouring to express the author's intention as fully as it is possible at this stage. There may not be time to hold two readings of the whole play at one session, especially following the conference. It will in this case be more advantageous to do Act 1 twice, than Act 1 and Act 2 once each.

These readings will be almost valueless if the players use ordinary conversational tones as if they are reading to each other in strict privacy! The producer *must* insist on the cast "pitching" their voices exactly as if they were on the stage with an audience present. This is not to be construed as an order to shout, nor does it entail the least vocal strain. If the voice is employed correctly, there is no more physical fatigue in "throwing" it than in indulging in the confidential mumblings so beloved by some professionals both in London and the Provinces.

Incidentally, I would stress that this inflexible rule about "pitching" the voice as if on the stage of a theatre applies equally to every rehearsal, from beginning to end. How ridiculous it is for a player to imagine that he or she can characterize and portray any kind of emotion, whether it be in farce, comedy, or tragedy, in a private and confidential voice. He is in worse trouble when he suddenly awakens to the knowledge that he is about to face several hundred people in a theatre and must suddenly begin to use an altogether different voice in order to be audible! On the other hand, if he has pitched his voice from the beginning, he continues thus when the public performances open, apart from any slight vocal adjustment that he finds later is demanded by the acoustics of the particular theatre.

Whenever I have encountered inaudibility at a drama festival I have invariably discovered that this rule has not been adopted.

"Tempo" and "Climax"

Little can be said to the cast on these points until rehearsals begin. It will be useful at the conference, however, to give general indications of major variations in *tempo*, and to stimulate imagination by discussing the more exciting climactic "moments."

The principal objects of the conference and preliminary readings should now have been achieved—the establishment of mutual understanding, the frank exchange of views, a homogeneity of approach, and a general unanimity of conception of the author's intention.

CHAPTER VI

INTERPRETATION AND TREATMENT

BEFORE we enter the rehearsal room for the first time, let us discuss plays in general, their interpretation, and varying forms of "treatment."

The importance of placing the play in the right category—farce, light comedy, satirical comedy, domestic drama and so on has already been stressed. At the same time, study of the script has enabled us to estimate the "key" of the composition. What do we really mean by "key"? Most plays contain both "dramatic" and "comedy" elements, often sharply contrasted. Does this mean that some parts of the play are in one "key" and others in another? No. A play is like a symphony composed in one key, and yet possesses variations of mood, which are expressed by variations of treatment. The "key" of the play refers more to its general or "over-all" purport. That is to say, the author intends, in satire, to be lightly, wittily, even flippantly satirical, or bitterly, even searingly so. In other words, his play may be sheer entertainment—or a cautery. A comedy or a drama may be a sincere commentary on life and human nature, or it may depart from realism for "escapist" entertainment purposes, or in the direction of experimental "expressionism" or some form of fantasy to suit the author's special purpose. The essential thing is that he must not mix his *styles*, his work must be homogeneous in order to carry conviction. *and* the actor's treatment must be equally consistent. The mixing of styles in one play is frequently misunderstood. How is it, one may ask, that Sean O'Casey in, say, *The Plough and The Stars*, can switch us instantaneously from irrepressible laughter to terror and tears? Is this not mixing oil and water, or, to revert to the musical analogy, a change of "key"? The answer is, again, "No," for in all the scenes, regardless of *the nature of the emotion aroused*, the *degree* of "realism" is the same. Indeed, in most of his plays O'Casey succeeds in swinging from tragedy to something *akin* to farce and back, and to and fro, again and again, without the least danger of "losing" his audience—always providing the acting is right. At the zenith of his success, his most criticized (and, perhaps his least convincing) play was *The Silver Tassie* in which he alternated between bitter realism and "expressionism." Whether the various forms of experimental drama appeal to one or not is immaterial. The point is that here we have an almost classic instance of the failure of a great playwright to "change key" within the fabric of his play.

Treatment Control

The producer of comedy will find that his most common problem will be the tendency of his players to tip over the edge into the realm of farce. This arises mostly from a natural anxiety to "get laughs." In light comedy, the writer, too, is faced with the constant temptation to exaggerate the fun. His responsibility is to decide whether he is going to write a comedy or a farce—and to stick to his decision! Characters have a way of "running away" from their authors, so this problem is not so easy to solve as it sounds. When this has occurred, the producer and player must combine in restoring a unanimity of treatment so far as this is possible. Similar situations will face them in "dramatic" plays. The precise quality and degree of "naturalism" must be gauged and adhered to strictly. "Melodrama" in the old sense of the term does not often make its appearance to-day—except to be burlesqued. But in "thrillers" or other forms of "escapist drama," a certain departure from realism (strictly controlled) is permissible.

"Naturalism"

It is necessary to be quite clear from the start exactly what is meant by this term. It is applied to the treatment of every type of play which (whether drama or comedy) is intended to be a realistic reflection of, or commentary on, life as we see it.

This is not a textbook on the technique of acting, which is analysed in another volume in this Series. It is, however, worth pointing out here that in the sphere of "realism" it is not the player's business to "be" natural. But it most certainly *is* the player's function to *create the illusion of nature*, a different and far more complex task—and it provides the reason why "technique" is required!

Acting is, indeed, the art that conceals art; the whole business of acting is the creation of illusion. From the first moment, when the curtain rises, the audience must be transported to another, yet "real," world, and must only be subconsciously aware that they are in a theatre and that it is all "make-believe."

It is strange yet true that if the actor behaves *really*

naturally (i.e., as he does, or would do, in private life) he is immediately unconvincing as a "naturalist" actor. It is only when he is *acting* (within the true limits of technically artistic "naturalism") that he deceives his audience into thinking that he is "being natural." Any departure from this method must be not in the direction of "private" naturalism, but in that of the particular artistic treatment that the character and type of play demand.

The "Shape" of a Play

It is a generally accepted principle that in the majority of plays the first act is mainly "exposition," the second concerned with the development of the conflict (with the highest point of climax at the "curtain"), and the third with the resolution of the problem, or some other satisfactory form of termination. At the same time, the curve of interest and excitement is not uniform in every play. These may be imagined as graphs plotted like temperature charts, in which will be observed a marked difference between the patients! Moreover, the producer will note the balance between the intensity of comedy and the intensity of drama as between scene and scene. Reference must be made to it here since it plays an important part in gauging "shape." The producer, at periodic "runs through," must keep a sharp eye on the maintenance of shape and balance. It brings us, moreover, to an important discussion on:

How Emotional Effect is Produced

Almost anyone with a minimum of musical knowledge can stand up and beat three, or four, in a bar with a baton; but that is not *conducting*. It requires little skill to "hold a script," read out stage directions, and "prompt." That is not *producing*.

If you watch a fine conductor you will observe how at one moment he is suppressing the "brass," at another giving a "lead" to the "woodwind," urging his orchestra to a *crescendo* or an *accelerando*, soothing them to *piano* or *pianissimo*, or ensuring that a *rallentando* is not too soon, too late, or too marked.

This is where the "conductor" analogy is most applicable to the producer, for emotional effect both in individual and collective acting is achieved more by variation of *tempo*, and of tone, than, perhaps, any other means. There are no rigid rules, and dogmatism is dangerous. As a general principle, however, it will be found that excitement, fury, terror, increasing "fun," and farcical confusion are normally accompanied by a heightened *tempo*, a quickening of pace in speech and action. The doomful moments, passages of pathos, periods of philosophic exchange, comedy that derives from indolence, are examples of treatment that are marked by a relatively slow *tempo*. There will be exceptions in both categories. For instance, a "conspiratorial" incident in one play will need quick, sharp playing. The dialogue of this passage will probably be crisply written and "liney," that is to say, composed of brief speeches of only a few words each. In another play a conspiratorial passage will call for a relatively slow *tempo*, and there is a likelihood here that individual speeches will be more amply written than in the former example.

Another general principle is that the quicker and more exciting the scene the greater the volume of vocal tone.

For instance, we all speak more loudly when we are angry than when we are kind. We are all inclined to raise our voices when we are convulsed with laughter and to lower them when we are sad. Again, there will be exceptions. To employ the former example (of conspiracy), the pitch of voice will be governed chiefly by the likelihood, or otherwise, of the conspirators being overheard! The various changes in, and combinations of, pace and tone are matters, primarily, for the producer's direction.

Tempo—Real and Apparent

There is one fundamental truth about pace that every producer must learn himself and impart to all his players. It is this: there is a profound difference between *real time* and *stage time*. That is to say, a pause, or a piece of action unaccompanied by dialogue ("silent bus.") which occupies five or six seconds of actual time seems, to the *audience*, to have occupied anything from eight to twelve seconds, according to the prevailing mood, but certainly much more than the *real* time. It follows, therefore, that whatever illusion the player wishes to create, his pause, or "silent bus.," must occupy less *real* time than the apparent time. This is why cues must be "picked up" so quickly, and dialogue "stream-lined." A hesitation of less than one second seems like a second or more, and the general impression on the audience is that of lagging, disjointed conversation. The same principle must be applied to the pace of delivery of the dialogue itself, which does not mean an excuse, however, for "gabbling" or faulty articulation. Variations in *tempo* and tone, then, are primary factors in creating emotional effect or interpreting lines. There are also "vocal punctuation," the pause, correct distribution of emphasis, and physical action to be considered, but these will be dealt with in Chapter VII in which the successive stages of rehearsal method are treated.

There is, however, one last injunction on the *producer's* attitude towards the player's craft: Do not forget that there are two major and distinct elements in acting—the "conception" and the "projection." If you are to extract the maximum value from your author's work, you must impress this truth upon your cast. A comedian can paint his nose red and put on a comic hat—it does not make him funny. It makes him look funny—for a time. Sooner or later the attitude of the audience will be: "Well, come on, now make us laugh." And if the fun is not inside the comedian, ready to bubble out—he is lost!

So, too, in tragedy. The player must "have that within which passeth show," and not only "the trappings and the suits of woe." The first, imaginative element, is essential to the second, which is largely a matter of the physical mechanics of acting. This is not to say that the player suffers the emotion (either comic or tragic) in the moment of acting. His personal emotional experience occurs during the process of conception. It colours, but must not control, his actual work upon the stage.

CHAPTER VII

REHEARSAL METHOD—1. MECHANICS

NO producer should embark on rehearsals without having planned a schedule of the work that he intends to cover at each, and a copy of this must be sent to every player as soon as possible after the final meeting of the casting committee.

The schedule of rehearsals varies for every play. It is governed chiefly by the following considerations:

(1) Nature of play.
(2) Size of cast.
(3) Total duration of rehearsal period.
(4) Evenings when all the cast are available, and when some are not.
(5) Relative importance, or difficulty, of various scenes.
(6) Existence of "crowd" scenes, where "supers" and numbers of small part players are involved.
(7) Various local conditions and difficulties.

Obviously, when casting, the standpoint of the producer and the committee must be "the show comes first." At the same time, this consideration may make some concessions imperative. There may well be instances of casting so nearly ideal that withholding a limited degree of compromise about rehearsal nights would be the height of folly.

Unfortunately, amateur rehearsals of a straight play are frequently stretched over far too long a period. Operatic productions rarely exceed four weeks. A section of a rehearsal schedule should read something like this:

TEMPLETOWN THESPIANS

"THE MELTON MYSTERY"

SCHEDULE OF REHEARSALS

Date	*Time*	*Place*	*Act*	*Remarks*
Mon., 10th Jan.	7.15	St. Peter's Hall.	ALL in ACT 1. Positions, etc.	
Tues., 11th Jan.	7.15	St. Peter's Hall.	ALL in ACT 1.	
Thur., 13th Jan.	7.15	Corner Café.	PRINCIPALS in ACT 2, Sc. 1. Positions.	"BARKER," "GEORGE" and SUPERS not required.
Fri., 14th Jan.	7.15	St. Peter's Hall.	ALL in ACT 2. Sc. 1, Sc. 2. Positions, etc.	FULL ACT 2 Cast.
Mon., 17th Jan.	7.15	St. Peter's Hall.	ALL in ACT 3. Positions.	
Tues., 18th Jan.	7.15	St. Peter's Hall.	ALL in ACT 3.	
Thur., 20th Jan.	7.15	Corner Café.	ALL in ACT 2. Sc. 2 only.	*Note.*—"BARKER," "GEORGE," and SUPERS must attend.
Fri., 21st Jan.	7.15	St. Peter's Hall.	FULL CO. for ACT 1, ACT 2, Sc. 1, ACT 3.	ABOVE NOT REQUIRED.

Later sections will show entire evenings devoted to "special scenes," in which only a few players are involved, others where the entire cast are required on a date that may appear to be surprisingly early. These features will be due, respectively, to the need to conquer difficult scenes (i.e., difficult to interpret emotionally or involving complicated and detailed "business") and the value of periodic revisions or "runs through" to enable the whole company to keep the entire play in perspective and fresh.

The preparation of the rehearsal schedule demands considerable thought, since upon its perfect planning depends the "building up" of the production in stages of ideal sequence so that no section of the play is neglected while others become "stale" by over-rehearsal.

The First Rehearsal

In an amateur production the earliest rehearsals may be attended only by those of the cast who are concerned in the act under consideration. As soon as the play is well under way, however, the entire cast should be present, whenever possible, in order that everyone may get the "shape" of the play and adjust accurately their stage relationship to the characters with which they are associated and their individual "places" in the story.

The cast is assembled for the first rehearsal. Each member has his, or her, copy of the play *and a pencil.* Before their arrival, the S.M. and A.S.M. have marked out the limits of the scenery, perhaps with chalk lines, or with "walls" of chairs with which the rehearsal-hall may be provided. The exits are clearly indicated by gaps between chairs, and the furniture must be

Another production of "Othello;" this one by the Wayne University Theatre, Detroit, Michigan, 1954.
Courtesy ANTA

The small stage of Westminster College's theatre was used for their production of "Othello" in 1952.
Courtesy ANTA

represented as nearly as possible by tables, chairs, and so on.

Either the S.M. or one of the A.S.M's will be in constant attendance on the producer and provided with a copy of the play and the ground plan. The cast will first gather around the producer, *facing the set*, with the ground plan before them, the scene is carefully described, and points of confusion are cleared up by question and answer.

As soon as the producer is confident that his players visualize the scene, they retire to seats conveniently near yet clear of the set, and are enjoined to watch and tc keep reasonably quiet. Here it is as well to mention tha incessant "giggle and chatter" is forbidden. On th other hand, a rehearsal-room is not a Trappist monas tery. A moderate amount of more or less inaudibl conversation (in the remotest corners of the room! should distress only the most temperamental of prc ducers. At the same time, the more the players ar encouraged to listen and to watch (and thereby to *learn*), the less garrulous they will become—even the females! Much will depend upon how interesting the producer can make the rehearsal.

At the first rehearsal, the cast is occupied with Act I. The players are taken through their entrances, major movements, and exits, reading their dialogue in clear, well-pitched voices. The players make marginal notes of any revisions of movement, etc., differing from what is printed in the script. These notes must be made at the time, and the S.M. and the A.S.M. will also note them if they are adjustments of what the producer has already written in his "marked" script.

At present, the producer does not trouble his players with technical faults in acting, or deviations from the agreed basic characterization. As the rehearsal proceeds he will, so far as appears wise, deal with "major business," but usually in a first session the broad "positions and movements" of a single act should be mastered as thoroughy as possible, and no more.

I advocate strongly the completion of "positions and major business" of the entire play before any "interpretive" rehearsals are embarked upon. When these latter begin for each successive act, only a "re-cap." on positions should be necessary.

Another feature that always pays a dividend is the compression of the purely "mechanical" rehearsals into a period of nearly consecutive nights. Even if the interpretive rehearsals must be more "spread over" (though this must be avoided as far as possible) it does assist the cast to "get into" the play if the positions are mastered during an intensive and closely-knit series of rehearsals.

As the mechanics are conquered, the producer must begin to introduce elements of characterization. I remind the reader that, from the first session, the players have read their parts with well-pitched voices. This habit facilitates considerably their early attempts at characterization and, indeed, before long they interpret to some extent unconsciously, and the "theatre pitch" of their voices is almost "second nature" to them.

On the other hand, what the producer will have most in mind at this stage will be the perfection, or otherwise, of his marked script! He will discover (but must not be too dismayed) that it is one thing to visualize a group, a stage picture, or a series of movements in private, and to devise it on paper, and quite another when his players are endeavouring to reproduce his script in action. He may note some instances of "masking," a character here and there may not be in an ideal position for a verbal exchange with another, or, an entire picture may prove to some extent impracticable because of some subsequent action for which provision has not been made.

Terms Applicable to Movements

The producer will find it most helpful if he employs, in direction, the accepted stage terms for different kinds of movement. The cast must be made familiar with these:

CROSS. This term is applied to a definite crossing of the stage either from one side to the other or at least a marked change of position. It is commonly associated in the player's mind, also, with quickness of movement, although the expression is equally accurate when applied to a slow crossing of considerable length.

An example would read: "GEORGE *enters up L, hesitates, then crosses to the safe down R, and unlocks it.*"

MOVE. This denotes a position change of lesser length, perhaps of anything down to three or four paces. Although the word has no connexion with *speed*, many players appear to associate it with a relatively slower pace. In acting editions, however, it is more or less customary to indicate the required speed to be applied to a "move."

Examples:

"MURIEL *moves to RC, checks, and stares at* ROBERT."
"*He moves slowly to the piano, sits, and begins to play.*"
"*She moves quickly up C, and tears aside the curtain.*"

Probably none of the above instances involves a change much greater than half the width or depth of the stage.

BREAK. This usually indicates a movement of a character *away* from another to indicate some form of antipathy or a desire not to face the other character when replying. It is applied also to an UP-stage or DOWN-stage movement to change a grouping, or to bring about a clear line between two characters which the character that "breaks" was intercepting. It is a short movement and usually associated with relatively slow pace.

Examples:

"*He breaks a little R, turns, and addresses* ALICE."

"*She breaks up-stage, and turns to the piano.* PETER *and* HILDA *exchange significant smiles.*"

EASE. This is the slightest movement of all. It is usually applied to little more than an adjustment of position. It may be two or three paces or much less. As an example, suppose that PAUL is standing close to the R arm of a settee. The stage direction might read:

"PAUL *eases to below the settee, looks coldly at* BELLA, *and sits.*

PAUL. Very well. Tell me."

Another example:

"*She eases a pace towards him, looks him up and down, and then, quite suddenly, laughs.*"

Again, a player will frequently "ease" a pace down stage of another in order that, a few moments later, he may make a clean cross below the other for an exit or some other purpose. An amateur cast will soon learn to associate these terms with the type and extent of movement, and act accordingly.

The extent to which "business" is introduced at the earliest rehearsals must depend on the producer's discretion. At first, nothing should be done that interferes with the player's mastery of movement while still reading his lines. Sitting and rising must be included, also hand shaking and "miming" of major business. Eating and drinking with props should be omitted, but introduced immediately the members of the cast are independent of their scripts. I find it advisable to use every possible prop, however, at the earliest possible stage; I also insist on miming the opening and closing of doors from the beginning. The preliminary rehearsals afford (after the positions have been blocked in) excellent opportunities for instructing the less experienced players how to "make an entrance," "make an exit," and the elements of "footwork."

The important thing at this juncture is to lay a good foundation and no more. The sounder the basic work, the quicker and smoother the successive stages will prove to be.

CHAPTER VIII

REHEARSAL METHOD—2. PRELIMINARY INTERPRETATION

AS the early rehearsals proceed, problems of position, grouping, and movement are solved, and action is gradually elaborated. While "mechanics" are being completed, the producer must have the following factors well in mind:

(*a*) Dramatic domination—a subject already discussed;
(*b*) Positioning for "conviction" in playing;
(*c*) Grouping with a view to *subsequent* movement and change;
(*d*) Aesthetic value of the "stage picture."

Little more need be said about (*a*). The producer will soon see for himself how true are the principles set forth in Chapter III on this subject. He will discover, too, how his players feel dominant, or the reverse, according to the positions allotted to them for the delivery of certain lines. Here it may be stressed that nothing is more helpful to an amateur player than to be asked how he feels when speaking a line in one position compared with another. By stimulating imagination thus, he acquires a useful quality of "actor's discrimination," which teaches him not only how to convey domination but also how to portray subservience too!

(*b*) It is difficult to play important scenes convincingly when grouping is "untidy." This is a defect that an audience is quick to sense, although unable to name it. An excess of formality, an obviously contrived picture, is the other extreme, and no less a blunder. Scenes of importance and of any appreciable length between only two characters cannot be acted with conviction when the players are separated by almost the entire width of the stage. Frequently I have seen this serious fault committed, when, say, a long quarrel is enacted with RICHARD by the fireplace extreme R, and VERA at the window extreme L! The reason for the failure of this positioning is simple. At the rise of the curtain the eyes of the audience are directed instinctively and collectively to centre stage. They immediately switch to that stage feature which has the maximum visual attraction, but throughout the play the C area will always be that towards which they will unconsciously *wish* to look. Now, if dialogue is tossed to and fro between extreme R and extreme L the heads and eyes of the audience soon resemble those of the spectators at a Wimbledon Tennis Championship, with the result that they not only lose the significance of each line but *also fail to catch the reactions of the actor to whom it is spoken.* Antipathy, it is true, is often marked by a separation of the participants—but *not* to the most remote corners of the room! Indeed, a scene of recrimination must frequently involve an approach of the characters to each other, particularly if the quarrel terminates in violence. Conversely, a sympathetic scene necessitates proximity of the characters. In a love scene the young lady may, at some point, "break slightly R or L" in modest confusion—but sooner or later the male pursuer will pursue, especially if the incident is to close happily with an embrace! The producer will encounter numerous variants of these examples, and by a process of reasoning will rapidly acquire the knack of appropriate treatment.

(*c*) This is a consideration that I treated as an example of script-marking in Chapter III. Its complexity and importance will be manifest as rehearsals proceed.

(*d*) The necessity for "aesthetic value in stage pictures" will depend largely on the nature of the play. It will be least apparent in modern "naturalistic" plays, though not, I hasten to add, entirely absent. I would say, rather, that the beauty of the "pictures" in such a play must have a greater "apparent unconsciousness" than in any other.

The need for beauty in grouping and movement will increase with the poetic, or the spiritual, qualities of the play, or any other aesthetic content. Historical plays, plays in verse, fantasies, and religious plays are all likely to demand great beauty not only of costume, scenery, and lighting, but also in the formal arrangement of the characters.

Here, however, I must warn the producer strongly against the temptation to be excessively and consciously "formal." As a general principle, the movement and resultant "picture" should in itself be an expression (or an enrichment of the expression) of the purport of the scene. Nothing destroys the spiritual quality of a scene more surely than to have it expressed wholly or partially by movement and grouping that has obviously been rehearsed so carefully (and excessively) that it looks like just one more—and faultless—rehearsal.

Admittedly, there must be no fumbling, no hurried re-adjustment of an error, no glaring technical fault—*but it must look as if the players are doing it for the first time.*

More obvious formality is permissible in scenes of ritual and ceremony, where precedence, position, and movement are governed by custom, tradition, rank, or religious or "national" significance. In these matters the producer must use his own discretion and knowledge of the ceremonial purport.

Speech and Action

The producer is now free to pay increasing attention to how lines are spoken and how speech is blended with action and "business." Distribution of emphasis (the choice of the correct word or words to be stressed in each phrase), vocal punctuation, variation of *tempo* and tone—all these must begin to concern him at this stage. Nor must he lose sight of balance in "personality value," balance of scene with scene, and the maintenance of the "general character" of the play.

Members of the cast, at this stage, should be more or less independent of their "books." Some players are natural "quick studies," some slow. Some (and not only amateurs) are wilfully careless and lazy. Since the producer will discover the frequency with which "any excuse is better than none," he will usually find it best to be less merciful about memorizing lines than almost anything else! Nor is memorization confined to lines; movement and action must be implanted in the mind even before the dialogue. Many players remember lines by their position on the set on which they have to deliver them, even by minor actions that sometimes accompany them. This is a sound method.

To speak lines at rehearsal as they will be delivered ultimately is an effective aid to memorization.

The players must also from this point onwards develop their emotional interpretation freely, not only for their own sakes but also for those of their fellow players, so that the collective effort may achieve homogeneity and a perfect "ensemble."

Again I warn the producer against the player who "never gives a performance" until the final rehearsal. The producer who has been and continues to be weak about this individual is heading straight for disaster. He is not acting in the best interests of the show, and is repaying the *loyal* members of his cast but poorly.

If the rehearsal schedule has been competently plotted, the play soon takes shape. It will be well to spend an occasional session on a "run-through" *with the minimum interruption by the producer.* Nothing stimulates self-confidence in amateurs more than "going through the whole play" at a fairly early stage. Do not withhold this opportunity too long. It rarely fails to pay a dividend in enthusiasm and smoothness of performance.

All amateurs suffer from an occasional "dreadful" rehearsal. The "run-through" with a silent producer is the finest remedy. If the players show up well, it is a tonic; if they do not, the far-seeing producer will convert disaster into a spur to greater effort. An ounce of encouragement is worth a ton of recrimination.

CHAPTER IX

REHEARSAL METHOD—3. INTERMEDIATE

THE producer is entering his busiest period. Chief among the points now demanding his attention are:

(1) Final decisions on movement and "business."
(2) Development of emotional interpretation.
(3) Detailed tuition in acting technique.
(4) Special attention to "weak spots."
(5) Settlement of all problems with staff on scenery, furniture, props, costume, lighting, etc.

This stage of the production must be completed within a reasonable time during which rehearsals must be as *frequent* as possible. One rehearsal should be enough for (1) and members of the cast must realize that they are individually as responsible for accuracy under this heading as they are for lines. Further, it must be impressed upon them that the word "mechanics" does not imply the creation of a "mechanical" effect; on the contrary, this element of acting is fundamental to emotional expression, and must possess an apparent spontaneity no less than that evinced in the delivery of the dialogue. In short, (1) is inseparable from (2) which is concerned chiefly with:

The Interpretation of Dialogue

At this stage, with a relatively inexperienced company, I make it a rule to devote two entire rehearsal sessions (preferably on consecutive days) exclusively to this subject. (I assume that my reader privately regards the dramatic society for which he produces as a temporary school for actors.)

At these two rehearsals all remaining faults in the *distribution of emphasis* must be eliminated. Many players fail to appreciate that a word wrongly stressed can completely reverse the meaning of a phrase! Judging by drama festival observations, I am convinced that this is the most common and most glaring fault in interpretation by speech.

The *nuances* of intensity (and restraint) in speech must also be adjusted at these sessions. With these the variation of pace and tone, vocal punctuation, and the deliberate "pause" are intimately linked. These matters are included in acting technique (3) in addition to :

Movements, Action, and "Business"

The basic principles should have been imparted at the preliminary rehearsals and should now require no more than final correction and polish. After this stage there should be no necessity to instruct any of the players on foot movement, on how to "carry" himself, or with which hand he receives a "prop" from, or hands one to, another player, and so on. The finer shades of facial expression, "eye-play," and gesture must now be fixed.

The producer's greatest problem with an amateur company will often be the difficulty of convincing his cast that these minor details are essential parts of the show *and must not be varied or omitted at any subsequent rehearsal or performance.* Only when they have become almost instinctive will they achieve and retain spontaneity.

Two sessions will serve to reveal any weak spots that have not impressed themselves on the producer at previous "runs-through." It cannot be too strongly urged that their elimination must be achieved no later than at this stage of the production. If this involves additional private tuition for one or two of the "backward" players, now is the time to give it.

Throughout the intermediate rehearsals "props" must be used—cups and saucers, glasses, telephones, revolvers, letters, telegrams, "swords," etc. Not all that must be used eventually will be available, but substitutes must resemble "the real thing" as closely as possible. The use of actual food (in the most suitable stage forms) is extremely important. Stage eating and drinking need to be completely convincing and must be practised with edibles that can be consumed with ease and grace.

The aim of the plotted rehearsal schedule is to ensure that the essential work is tackled in proper sequence from foundation to roof. Play production should not be embarked upon haphazardly. Floors come before tiles; wall paper, enamel, and chromium door furniture last! We find ourselves, then, applying a fifth analogy —a producer is the architect of the building.

Staging the Play

Between rehearsal sessions the producer should discuss staging requirements with his staff. Every problem of scenery, furniture, props, costume, and lighting must be solved not later than two weeks before production. The producer should avoid, if possible, accepting the "next best thing," insist on the impossible as long as possible—and then submit to the minimum of compromise with charming grace! This must not be taken, however, as a simplification of his problems. On the contrary, he must have the knowledge and ability to suggest solutions, alternatives, and improvisations and to see that they are carried out.

I remind the producer who may assume that he will enjoy occasional leisure at this stage, that some final tuition in make-up will probably be necessary—unless he has a deputy instructor. There will also have to be visits to the theatre to clear up points and to keep an eye on staff progress, and committee members may ask troublesome questions!

Prompt Copy

At this stage the prompt copy should be complete, fully annotated, and ready for use in the theatre. If, as sometimes occurs in amateur productions, it is the duty of the prompt to warn "Lights" for the lighting changes, the copy must be marked "WARN LIGHTS" in *red ink* a few speeches before each cue, and the cues themselves marked "LIGHTS—GO" in green, with an arrow-head or a big green dot.

Similarly, the call-boy's copy must be marked with warnings in red for each member of the cast at points in the script that allow ample time for every call to be given and obeyed.

The period ends with a full "run-through" uninterrupted by the producer, who delivers an "adjudication" at the end. The play now "lives," and the company is ready for the most exciting stage of the production.

CHAPTER X

REHEARSAL METHOD—4. THE FINAL STAGES

PRODUCER and company must regard all rehearsals from now onward as being, virtually, performances. True, they will not have that final collaboration, the presence of an audience, which alone can complete the creation. None the less, the rehearsals must be treated as performances, with firm adherence to interpretation by word and deed, not even the least point being left to "inspiration on the night." In short, the cast must perform (and behave) as if an audience were present.

The producer should view his "creation" in perspective and decide whether he has achieved "shape," "balance," and "climax." Is the comedic element of this scene or that sufficiently brought out? Does it, on the other hand, incline to swamp the "drama"? Is SIR HENRY too strongly played—or is *he* just right but HARRIET lacking in personality value? Is that "pause and silent exit," immediately before the curtain of Act 2, a shade too long—or a little too quick? How are these elements likely to affect "audience control?" These are the questions the producer must ask himself now—and answer. Experience will assist him. Yet even with this—prophecy may prove fallible, for what producer or player can foresee with certainty audience reactions, which will probably vary. Yet, however unreliable speculation may be, the producer must stand or fall by his final directions.

The following are some of the matters that must now deeply concern him:

Attack: Nothing induces a loss of interest (and the creation of restlessness) in the audience more than the absence of crisp "attack" and a continual listlessness of treatment. There are numerous variants of "openings" to plays or acts. They range from the "empty stage and black-out" to the brilliantly lighted crowd scene with a babel of uproar. Yet every "opening," as soon as speech begins, can have some quality of "attack," however quiet, and this must be sustained (with variations of intensity) throughout. The gravitating voice, the sustained slowness of *tempo*, and indeterminate "sloppy" movement lull the audience and deaden interest.

Climax: Climactic moments of varying degrees of excitement coincide usually with the fall of the curtain on each act, but they occur also during the action. The relative heightening of each climax is one result of the application of the producer's skill—if the author has provided the written material out of which these moments may be created! In general the highest points of climax are at the "curtains," since the wise dramatist aims at leaving his audience in a state of expectancy during the intervals, wishing to know what "is going to happen next." There is, however, no inflexible law on this, since plays differ vastly in character and purport, but the producer must give careful direction as he conceives and gives significance to the author's intention.

Suspense is not confined to speculations that are made between the acts! It occurs during the traffic of the play, and may be achieved by varied means. The sensation of suspense may be aroused by the inscrutability of a single character, or by the mysterious behaviour and cryptic utterances of a group of players. Momentary suspense can be created by stillness and silence, which can be protracted if the "suspension" is *acted*: the stillness and silence must be clearly *intentional*, and as clearly *an expression of character and state of mind*. Otherwise the impression of an unfortunate lapse of memory may be conveyed.

Last Words on "Conducting": Our orchestral analogy now finds its maximum application. At each remaining rehearsal the producer must induce and control all the subtle variations of *tempo* and of tone. If he has built up the elements of his production in correct sequence, however, he will obtain ready response to his baton. After a few full rehearsals, with perhaps one or two "special scene sessions," the company is ready for:

The Dress Rehearsal: First, I emphasize the importance of having, if possible, the last three or four rehearsals on the stage of the theatre, with the scenery and furniture, if available, and certainly the actual props to be used during public performance. If the production is of a costume play, the producer must insist on the wardrobe being delivered in time for a dress parade and, on a subsequent evening, a "run-through" in costume before the full dress rehearsal.

At the dress parade members of the cast are fitted, any errors are noted and dealt with, and the players move about freely in order to get the "feel" of their costumes. They also receive final instruction on "how to wear" the dress of the period and, while in costume, practise the appropriate gestures. A short rehearsal of one or two brief scenes should be included. These measures reduce the awkwardness that is often apparent in players who have not worn their costumes until the first night.

At the dress rehearsal, the atmosphere in the theatre is, invariably, changed. There is "electricity" in the air. Both amateur and professional players are subject to its influence. The producer should be at his calmest. Nothing—the collapse of the pillared arch up L for Act I, the gash in the centre of the sky-cloth, the leading lady's tears!—should ruffle him. His imperturbability will communicate itself (eventually) to All Concerned. It should be sustained throughout the first-night and the entire run!

The region of the stage is the inviolable domain of the S.D. and/or the S.M. and his staff. The wise producer will leave them to it, and not invade it unless he feels certain, or has been told, that his presence is necessary.

Before the rehearsal there will have been a setting and lighting rehearsal. Every lighting cue will have been tried out, every lamp on the spot-bar adjusted for "tilt," the last colour changes will have been made, and the timing of every "fade in" and "fade out" rehearsed. Stage hands, or members of the staff will have acted as "stand-ins" so that the various acting area "pools" are positioned and angled with the utmost accuracy. "Lights" has been satisfied (we hope!) and is in supreme command of the switchboard.

On the pass-door, through which the players will

reach the stage at the proper time, the following injunctions are boldly worded:

STAGE

CAST AND STAFF ONLY

NO SMOKING ALLOWED

SILENCE

In each dressing-room, in the green room (if any) and in other prominent places, is displayed a set of rules. These must be crisply, though politely worded, and be implacably enforced, irrespective of the importance or the sex of the players.

These rules will include an absolute ban on smoking "back-stage," no conversation there above a whisper, and then only about necessities. Nor, before the rise of the curtain, will any player be admitted to the stage region unless summoned by order of the producer. A player infringing any of these rules should be dismissed to the dressing-room by the stage director or manager without reference to the producer. Only during the action of the play have members of the cast free admission to the stage and they must be made to realize that "conversation in the wings" *can* be heard in the auditorium as clearly, sometimes, as "dialogue off-stage."

No less important is the "NO SMOKING" order. Amateurs sometimes complain that they are being treated as children. My reply is that if Sir Laurence Olivier or Dame Sybil Thorndike obey these rules willingly and without loss of dignity, the Templetown

Thespians should be similarly obedient. In any event, I never relax the rules!

While members of the stage staff are completing the setting-up, and "Lights" is setting his opening lighting, the producer is supervising make-up, making a tour of the dressing-rooms, encouraging all, and soothing "nerves," if any are noticeable. He should never be far away from his own dressing-room at this time, especially after the "half-hour call." The players should have arrived at least one hour before curtain rise. In a big show, with a chorus, or a crowd, and particularly in a costume piece, the "make-up call" must be earlier for the majority. Frequently, for such productions a professional perruquier and make-up staff has been engaged; then a strict "make-up rota" must be arranged and kept.

Not later than the "quarter-hour call" the S.M. will send an A.S.M. to the producer with the crisp message, "The stage is ready, sir." Thereupon, the producer makes his way immediately to the stage, ground plan in hand, and, with the S.D. or S.M., will "pass stage."

The flats must coincide with the coloured chalk marks on the stage-cloth that were drawn as guides at the first setting-up. The back-cloth must have no wrinkles, wings must perfectly "mask-in" the back-stage area, "borders" must completely conceal the lighting battens and the top edges of the flats, every door must open with ease—and close firmly. There is no worse "technical hitch" than a badly operating door. The precise adjustment of furniture and the presence of every stage prop for the opening are checked.

Corrections and adjustments having been made, the

producer signifies his approval, checks his watch with the S.M., the call-boys go their rounds, and the musical director (if there is an orchestra), is given a signal at the proper moment to take his place in the orchestra pit.

The producer now goes in front, ready to watch the rehearsal, taking with him an A.S.M. or, perhaps, the S.M., with note-pad and pencil.

The S.D. (or S.M.) is now in full command on stage. Signals are given for "Stand by tabs," "House lights out," etc., and he is sufficiently familiar with the show to "take the tabs up" at the right moment. The opening players are on stage, or in the wings, as required, and—THE PLAY IS ON!

If a production has been built up properly, the dress rehearsal ought to be comparatively smooth. There will be blunders. Some player will "come on" minus a sword or a powder compact; a door, despite the check, will mysteriously open without human agency; a "black-out" won't happen, and even the prompter's voice may be heard. In a back stall (or the dress circle) the producer listens, listens, listens, whispering notes to the A.S.M., who records them in full. Only disaster will induce the producer to shout "STOP!" If this occurs, as soon as the problem is solved, the cast goes back to the nearest point that is helpful to a resumption.

An "adjudication" follows each act. If necessary, "bits and pieces" are taken over again to fix them clearly, only the players involved remaining; the rest retire immediately, and quietly, to their dressing-rooms.

As soon as the stage is clear of players, the stage hands "strike" the set—if there is a change—and the stage staff change or re-arrange furniture and props.

The routine for the succeeding acts is similar. Opportunity must be created for dealing with revisions or corrections of lighting and setting, all essential points having been noted at the rehearsal.

Have I painted too rosy a picture? I do not think so. Much depends on the "build-up" during the preceding weeks; also on the loyalty and the enthusiasm of the cast and staff. The producer must not forget that these qualities can be inspired largely by his own approach and labour.

CHAPTER XI

OF FIRST NIGHTS AND PLAYERS. OF PLAY-GOERS, OF PRODUCERS, OF PLAYWRIGHTS AND PLAYS

THE routine and discipline on first—and subsequent—nights are the same as for the dress rehearsal, except, perhaps, that discipline should be even more rigidly enforced.

Most of the cast, on the first night, will not be (apparently) so fatigued on arrival as the producer has probably feared! "First night excitement" differs subtly from that of the dress rehearsal. There is also a condition diagnosed as "first night nerves." Of these the producer must be wary, for there are two distinct brands—the genuine and the spurious. The former may be partly physical and partly the over-anxiety of a conscientious artiste to give the best possible performance. This is successfully treated by calm encouragement and comradeship. The latter (easy to recognize if you have studied the "sufferer" during the rehearsal period) is just "put on" to prove the possession of an "artistic temperament"—even "artistic genius!" It can be ignored—until signs of spreading infection appear. Then the culprit should be taken aside and informed that the exhibition is not impressive and must cease.

The producer's first duty on arrival at the theatre, is to go on stage, to see that all is well with his staff, and to solve any problems that have arisen. He will then visit the dressing-rooms, supervising make-up and encouraging the cast until called by the A.S.M. to "pass stage." This will not occupy all his time; there will be matters that claim his attention in his own dressing-room.

During the performance he will be on stage most of the time, ready to deal with any first-night crises. If all is going well and his staff is quite reliable, he should try to see some of the show from the front in order that later he may correct, revise, or admonish for the improvement of subsequent performances.

The S.M. will record the precise playing time of *each act*, and the producer (who knows how long these should be) will be in a position to tell the cast when they have played too slowly or too fast; there may have been failure to pick up cues smartly and the delivery of some lines may have flagged, or pauses may have been exaggerated and "silent business" protracted. The offending players must be firmly warned and instructed.

The cast will have been asked to leave the stage IMMEDIATELY, SWIFTLY, and SILENTLY at the fall of the curtain on Acts 1 and 2. The staff have, say, eight minutes in which to "strike and set" and object to players getting in their way! How right they are! "Inquests," if unavoidable, should be conducted in the dressing-room or postponed until after the show.

No visitors are permitted on any pretext whatever, before or during the show—which means also "during the intervals."

Finally, the cast will have been rehearsed for the curtain calls at the end of Act 3. The players already on stage, remain; the others, who are standing by in the wings, enter swiftly and silently when the curtain falls, and the entire cast quickly forms the pre-arranged line. The producer signals the tabs up and down smartly, once, unless the applause merits another "call." The wise producer is not niggardly in giving his company full public acknowledgement, but must cut any calls after the applause is "dead." The surest way to kill applause is to hesitate in taking the curtain up again, *or* by keeping it up too long. The players have been taught how to acknowledge applause with dignity and grace. This must be done impersonally; there must be no conscious "bowing and smiling" to individual members of the audience. The obeisances should be definite and from the waist, and accompanied by a quiet smile. Any exhibitions of physical exhaustion ("I have given my public *my all* to-night") or giggles or whispers are in the worst possible taste.

Once the curtain is finally "down" the producer should allow the cast to "simmer down" before dealing with any points of correction. He must, however, be smart enough to get these tackled before his players receive their "fans." These visits ought to be prohibited, along with "last-night bouquets," but alas! this seems to be quite impossible. I have found that the best solution is to summon the players on stage before they begin to remove their make-up and to change. Some of the "effervescence" has subsided, and no strangers are admitted. The proceedings can be brief but must open with a word of thanks *from the producer*! Who knows—they may close with a round of cheers for the Captain of the Ship! And so to bed.

Of Playgoers

By what standards are you to judge the artistic success of your production? By the applause—or your inmost conviction of what has been right and what has been wrong? If you are capable of ruthless self-criticism, the latter is the more valuable criterion. But do not ignore too readily the verdict of the "customers." True, they may not "like" a good play even when it is well done; they may not, perhaps, understand it. It may even be *below* their intellectual level. They may fail to laugh in the right place, and laugh when they should not. They will vary in this and in most other respects night after night! The public is unpredictable—and yet—how frequently just in appraisement! When it fails in reaction, discernment, and respect, there is nothing *you* can do. It is for the players to dominate their audience, and for you to ask yourself to what degree you have taught them *how* to do so, since one of the principal assets to be derived from technique is the power to employ the personality in "audience-control," for though the actor is the servant of the public he must also be its master. So, too, must the producer. He cannot stand aloof and say "they do not matter." They do. They are there to be led, wooed, and won. The measure of their praise will also be the measure of the producer's sincerity and skill.

Of Producers

A well known author-adjudicator once told me he divided producers into "those with beards and strangely tinted corduroys" and "those who bought safety razors and neat grey slacks." While admitting that there are variants of these extremes I knew what he meant.

Experience has taught me that the more colourful ones are found, usually, to have the least "work-a-day" knowledge of stagecraft. Among these are the "divinely inspired"—those who are born with all the answers. They disdain the honest carpentry of acting technique. Do not join their ranks. One producer-playwright stated publicly that "90 per cent of amateur productions were taking money under false pretences." This utterance was as stupid and cruel as it was untrue. It is for producers and players to refute the charge by first-rate craftsmanship on high quality plays, and for groups to turn chiefly to producers for counsel on the choice of play.

Of Playwrights and Plays

"What Does the Public Want?" There are many answers to this question, but none that satisfies everybody. If the professional managers knew, no play would fail. There is a good deal in the saying, "They will learn to want whatever they are given." The trouble is that just as a chocolate éclair is easier to chew than a mutton chop, so a light "escapist" entertainment is easier to assimilate emotionally and intellectually than a play of greater beauty and deeper meaning. It is wise to admit that there are many different publics, each capable of the appreciation of a different type and grade of play. Indeed, any group will support, in turn, widely varying kinds of plays. Both éclairs and mutton chops become monotonous in time!

Your choice of play will be governed by (*a*) the kind of work your drama group wishes to do; and (*b*) the particular public to which it hopes to appeal.

If a group wishes to be progressive and to do really

satisfying work, an unbroken series of replicas of West End successes is *not* the course to take. Even these when played should be of some aesthetic and intellectual quality, though not necessarily "highbrow." But a limitation of activities to the other extreme is likely to prove equally disastrous, artistically and financially. The markedly "non-commercial" plays are not always the best training material in elements of technique. Moreover, occasional more "popular" plays (of which you have no need to be ashamed!) will serve to create and increase a "following" for the group which can then proceed to interest its public in those works in which the group itself is most interested. Do not imagine, however, that there is any special virtue, for instance, in doing an "experimental" play because it is experimental.

Nor is a play great, or even good because it is written in verse, whether "rhymed", "free", or "blank." It is the quality of the poetry that matters. That transcends in importance the story and, perhaps, even the characters. This is certainly true of many of the plays of Shakespeare. (I often wonder why more amateurs do not produce Shakespeare. There is no finer dramatic education.)

Beware the "obscurantist" play—chosen by some in the vain hope of being, thereby, accepted as "intellectuals." Yet take care to ensure that those which seem obscure are really so before you reject them. It may assist you if you remember that the true obscurantist's defence of his "obscurity" is often more obscure than the obscurity of his plays!

The aim of the Amateur Theatre should be to present plays of beauty, of fresh approach, and new in form.

The Amateur has a duty, however, to make sure that the beauty is *real*, the freshness a sincere urge towards deeper significance in human expression, and the form no less compelling than what has gone before.

This is the cross-road at which every artist in every form of art stands to-day—the point of choice between the spurious and the true. There are so many *poseurs*, fakes, leaders of strange, pretentious cults; yet so many sincere workers labouring for something finer, more truthful, and more illuminating and longing to be recognized.

The dual function of the Amateur Stage as I see it, is not only to entertain (a good thing in itself) but also to contribute something of real and lasting value to the art of the theatre. To fulfil this, its technicians and artistes need sincerity, integrity, imagination, and skill.

From the producer perhaps more than any other, inspiration and craftsmanship spring. The burden is heavy, but it is worth shouldering, isn't it?

Shakespeare's "Julius Caesar" as presented in New York's Edison Hotel Arena Theatre. Note the overhead lighting, and the audience sitting within reach of the players.

Photo by Barrett Gallagher, Courtesy ANTA

A scene from "Romeo and Juliet," as presented at the American Shakespeare Festival at Stratford, Conn.
Courtesy ANTA

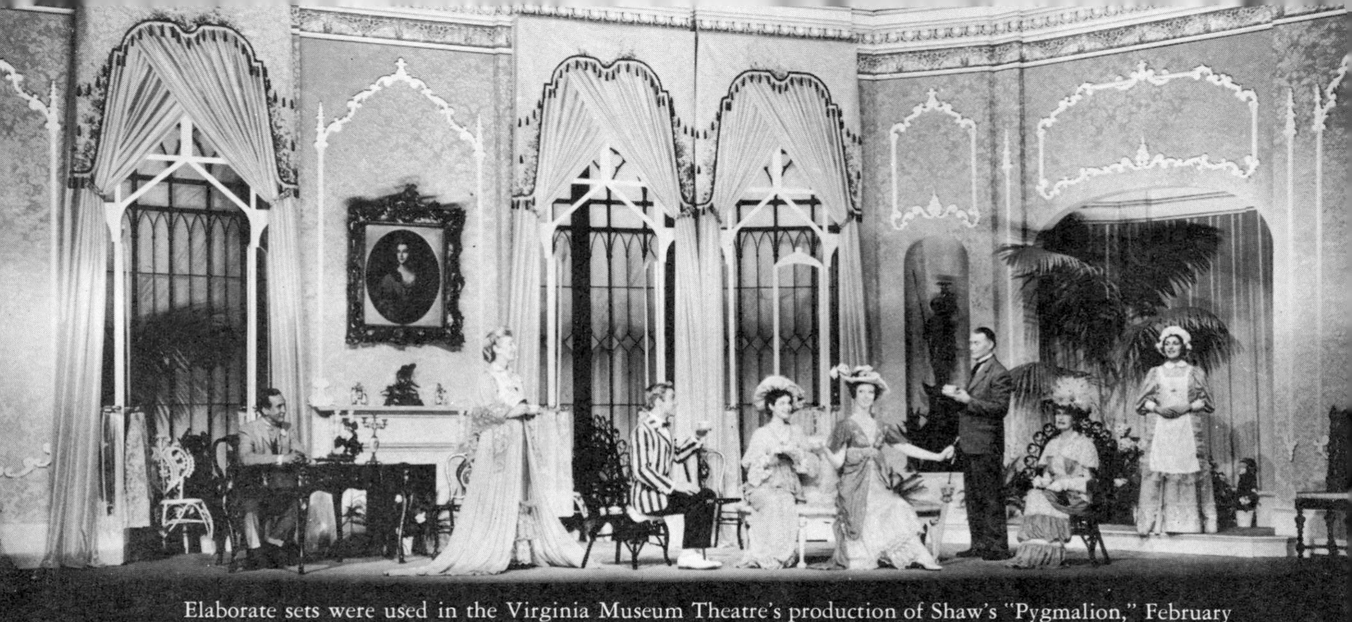

Elaborate sets were used in the Virginia Museum Theatre's production of Shaw's "Pygmalion," February 1962. Producer-Director was Robert S. Telford; William Ryan was the Designer.

Courtesy ANTA

A scene from T. S. Eliot's "Murder in the Cathedral," staged in the University Theatre of the University of Chicago.

Courtesy ANTA

Eliot's "Murder in the Cathedral" received a striking production at the "92 Theatre" of Wesleyan University, Middletown, Conn. The chorus is shown here.

Courtesy ANTA

Rehearsal of Act II of James Barrie's "What Every Woman Knows," as staged by the Sheboygan Community Players, Sheboygan, Wis.

Courtesy ANTA

University of Michigan student production of Shakespeare's "A Midsummer Night's Dream."
Courtesy ANTA

A tastefully designed set by George W. Schoenhut for the Capulet Ball Scene of "Romeo and Juliet," as produced by the Dartmouth Players.

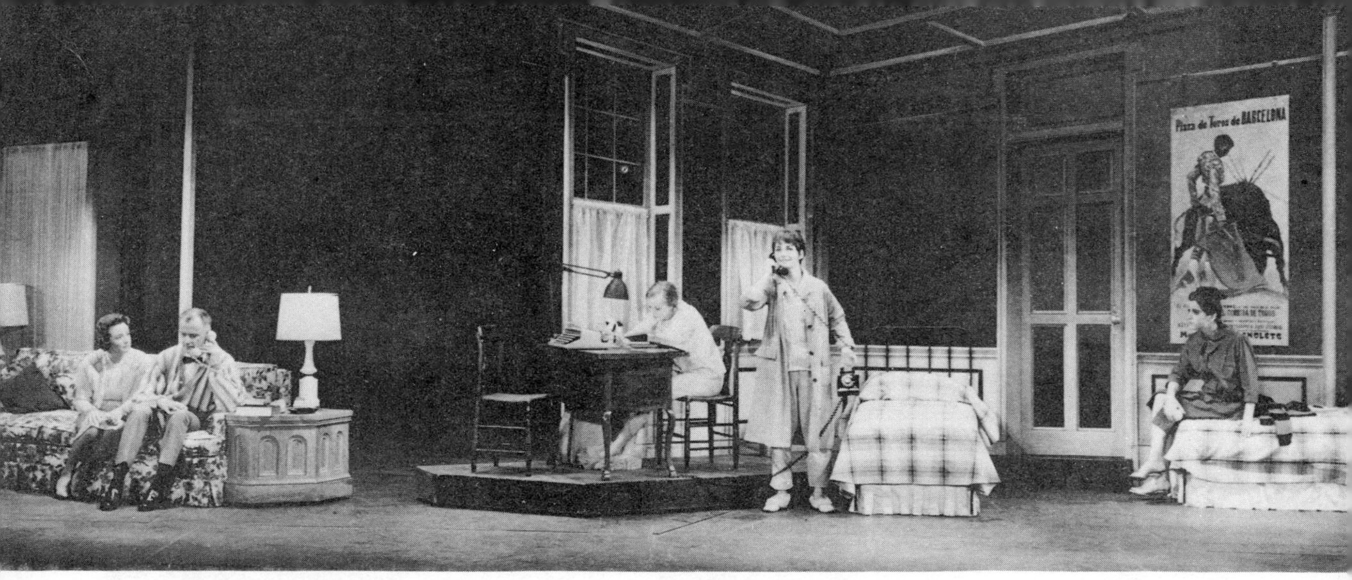

Imaginative staging was given to the Biltmore Theatre Broadway production of "Take Her, She's Mine," starring Art Carney, seen here at far left.

Photo by Eileen Darby-Graphic House

Striking design by Ralph Duckwall is evident in this scene from "Desire Under the Elms," by Eugene O'Neill, as produced by the University of Michigan.

George Crepeau was the designer of the University of Michigan's staging of Shakespeare's "Romeo and Juliet."

Courtesy ANTA

Elaborate, intricately designed set for the Catholic University's production of Shakespeare's "Julius Caesar."

Simple but effective is this set for "King Lear," as performed at the Mary Washington College, Virginia.
Courtesy ANTA

Wendel Josal designed the sets, Robert D. Moulton designed the costumes, for Shakespeare's "King Lear," produced by the University of Minnesota.

Courtesy ANTA

A typically fine setting is evident in this performance of "A Midsummer Night's Dream," at the American Shakespeare Festival, Stratford, Conn.

Courtesy ANTA

During a rehearsal of Shakespeare's "Julius Caesar" at the American Shakespeare Festival Theatre, Stratford, Conn.

Courtesy ANTA

Part II: STAGECRAFT

PREFACE

(Stagecraft)

by Harcourt Williams

ONCE I overheard a child say, as it looked gloomily at its square yard of allotted garden, "I do hate my hobby!" If to act as an amateur is to pursue a hobby, I wish that the word could lose its present implication of incompetence and revert to its original meaning. Whether one is a professional actor or an amateur it is essential that one should *love* one's "hobby."

The Amateur Stage, since its spectacular revival after the First World War, has done much for the English-speaking theatre and deserves to be taken seriously.

The authors of this book are under no misapprehension about the hard work involved in the practice of stagecraft. Their information is both lucid and exhaustive. Here the stage manager is the *deus ex machina*, the man who pulls the strings. Gordon Craig has insisted that the S.M. should be of supreme importance in the theatre, and deplored his fall from power when the modern "producer" made his entrance at the opening of the twentieth century.

One of the theatre's assets is illusion, or it was until we professional actors sold our heritage for a mess of potage cooked in Fleet Street and elsewhere. Our duty is to salvage what we can. It is good, therefore, to turn the pages of this book, dispassionately set out and designed neither to give away the tricks of the trade nor for uncritical "fans" and trivial seekers after "back-stage" gossip, but to appeal to the keen, bright-eyed, would-be workers in the theatre.

The general public, viewing the stage from the auditorium, have little conception of how businesslike and normal life behind the scenes must be. Consequently, those who enter it for the first time are apt to confuse the excitements of painting their faces and disporting themselves in antic costumes before the footlights with the very essence of acting.

Those, however, who approach the job seriously and are ready to renounce social pleasures if they interfere with its practice, also those who are prepared to accept the rigid discipline of the theatre and its inevitable disappointments, will experience the joy that is the crown of work well worth doing.

To achieve acting at its best all vanities must be discarded. Self-consciousness, self-satisfaction, and the foibles of egotism must be cast off, until, stripped bare like the stage when it is ready for the first rehearsal, the actor stands ready to accept the children of the author's imagination and to develop these in the light of his own experience.

LIST OF ILLUSTRATIONS

CHAPTER I

THE STAGE MANAGER

THE stage manager (referred to as S.M. throughout this book) is the man or woman who is responsible for the branch of amateur theatricals that is known as stagecraft. We must, therefore, define "stagecraft" as it is dealt with in this book.

Briefly, stagecraft deals with the *practical* side of all that is seen and heard when a play is presented to an audience, and includes costuming, make-up, and lighting. Here we are not concerned in detail with these three branches of stagecraft because (1) they are separately dealt with in this Series, and (2) our experience is that costumes and make-up are best left to the producer and cast alone—though when the S.M. comes to design his set he will need to know the colours of the costumes that will be worn so that he can work out his own colour scheme with these in mind. (See Chapter III.) All but the simplest of electrical lighting equipment will call for the services of an electrician. Usually, the layman will be able to receive instruction from the caretaker or electrician of the hall or theatre booked for the production; or the group may have its own electrician. In any circumstances, lighting will have to be taken into consideration by the S.M., if only to enable him to remind the producer of the limits of the effects that can be obtained. (For a few general principles of lighting, see Chapter V.)

There are, then, the stage itself, the set, properties, and effects. The set consists of the scenery as seen by the audience; properties include furniture and the various objects used throughout a performance; effects denotes the different means of producing noises on or off the stage and any other unusual visual features (rain, fog, wind, background music, etc.). Our point of view is that of the small dramatic group as distinct from the large, affluent, and highly organized society, which usually has its carpenters, property masters, décor designers, and electricians; in short, it has a "residential stage staff." The small society is lucky if it has one man to cope with all these tasks.

The Stage Manager

What are the qualities desirable in the small group's "omnibus" manager who often works single-handed, or with willing but untrained help? He should be practical, have an eye for method, a clear brain, and "mechanical sense." We do not suggest that he need be an engineer or a builder; but he should know when to use a screw and not a nail; a bolt and not a screw. He needs method and a clear brain because he may find he is the only member who does not suffer from producer's tension or actor's nerves at the dress rehearsal or the final performance. As such he is a valuable corrective. Ideally, he should be on good terms with his colleagues and capable of inspiring confidence and calm. If he has a sense of humour, he will help to make amateur dramatics a pleasure.

Function

What is the S.M.'s function in the small society? What is he expected to do, and how does he do it?

We have taken a typical example of the part played by an S.M. from the time the play is chosen, up to, and including, its actual public performance. Circumstances vary widely because of differing drama groups, stages, and general facilities. The keen S.M. soon devises his own tricks and methods.

A full-length play is assumed, but the general principles apply to the stage management of one-act plays. Firstly, the S.M. should be in evidence at the beginning of the production enterprise, i.e. when the play is chosen. He should be a member of the executive committee, be in a position to advise on the practical possibilities of staging the suggested play, and have a sound idea of the cost. To be able to do this he will need to read the play carefully and so bear in mind both the size of the stage that will be used and the facilities that will be available. The play with a single set throughout will be less troublesome than one that requires a complete change of scene. When a play has several different scenes a different approach is necessary; realism will have to be abandoned; only symbolical or suggested scenes will be possible. (See Chapter III.)

The possibilities of modifying and adapting a play to suit a small stage should not be overlooked. Careful study will reveal what set, properties, and effects are essential, and what can be omitted. Often the S.M. must exercise much ingenuity, but although a play may be cut, it must not be added to or altered.

When the play has been chosen, the S.M. is ready to tackle his first job—the preparation of his script.

CHAPTER II

PLANNING

Preparing the Script

TO stage-manage a play several notes will have to be made by the S.M. in relation to the text, actors' moves, lighting, effects, etc. These notes, together with the text of the play, are known as the "script." It should be regarded as a valuable document from the first. It is not always realized that a well-prepared script can make for smooth running, both at rehearsals and during the actual production to the public. It often happens that understudies are expected to be able to replace absent actors, and it should be possible for someone to take over from the S.M. should he be forced to drop out at a late stage; a clearly annotated working script is thus a safeguard.

The practice of scribbling notes all over a copy of the play is to be deprecated; to mark borrowed books is even more reprehensible. The copy of the play is usually in the form of a soft-covered volume, and from this the script is prepared. If the play is expensively bound, or forms one of a collection, the only really satisfactory method of dealing with it is to have it typed. The leaves of the play are interleaved with sheets of plain paper, and it facilitates working if the sheets are all on the left-hand side and the text of the play is on the right. To do this with printed copies two books are needed. The leaves are carefully separated from the binding, and by taking one from each book alternately they can be arranged in order and re-bound on the left side by means of punched holes threaded with tape or string. Stiff cardboard for the outer covers is necessary, for the script will receive hard wear.

By thus having the text constantly on the right and the notes on the left a ready scanning is made easier during re-

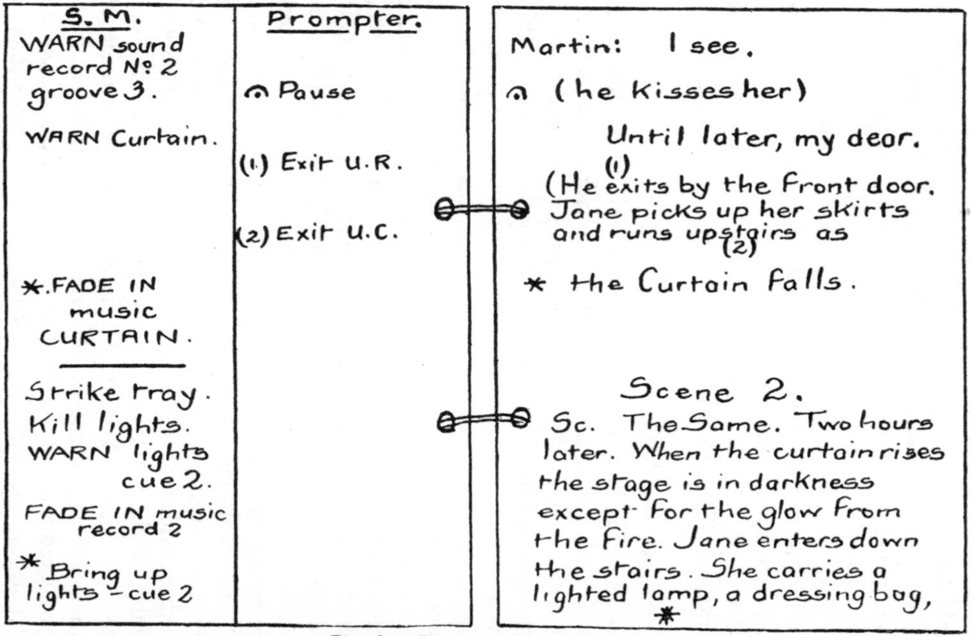

S. M.

WARN sound record No 2 groove 3.

WARN Curtain.

*. FADE IN music CURTAIN.

Strike tray.
Kill lights.
WARN lights cue 2.

FADE IN music record 2

* Bring up lights – cue 2

Prompter.

Pause

(1) Exit U.R.

(2) Exit U.C.

Martin: I see.

(he kisses her)

Until later, my dear.

(He exits by the front door. (1) Jane picks up her skirts and runs upstairs (2) as

* the Curtain falls.

Scene 2.

Sc. The Same. Two hours later. When the curtain rises the stage is in darkness except for the glow from the fire. Jane enters down the stairs. She carries a lighted lamp, a dressing bag, *

Fig. 1. Prompt Copy, Open.

hearsals and productions, but, if desired, the script can be prepared by using one copy only. Then the blank sheets will appear on alternate sides of it. A few extra sheets back and front will be found useful for general notes. The interleaving sheets should then be ruled in two columns, the left being for the S.M.'s notes, the right for the producer's moves (i.e. his instructions to the cast). (See Figure 1.) An added refinement is to number the speeches in the text, and if the producer and cast do likewise with their copies, a quick reference is available. (". . . go from speech 5, page 17 . . ." etc.)

"Vetting" the Text

This should be done in consultation with the producer. It consists of extracting the necessary information from the text. At the back of acting editions will usually be found a list of properties and furniture, properties being the various portable articles, such as cigarettes, books, etc., used by the performers. This list can be used, but, in addition, the play should be scrutinized, and the properties and furniture listed under three headings, Furniture, Stage Dressings, and Properties. Only those articles of furniture essential to the play should be listed, and the sources of supply should be noted as soon as possible (i.e. the firm from which it is to be hired, or the members of the society lending parts of their home). By stage dressings are meant the drapes, tablecloths, ornaments, etc., which are not moved during a scene and which may not be essential to the action (being used to "dress" the stage). Properties are further divided into two groups: stage properties, the responsibility of the S.M., and hand properties, for which the cast are responsible. As with the furniture, a note is made of where the stage dressings and properties are to be obtained. Special requirements for lighting and sound effects should also be noted at this stage, e.g. which effects will best be achieved manually (with wind machine, bells, coconut shells, etc.) and which will be better obtained by recordings.

On one of the blank pages at the front of the script should be drawn a ground plan of the setting of each scene, showing the position of the furniture, etc., each being marked clearly with the act and scene. It is also a good idea for the beginner to "square off" one of these plans in order to show to which part of the stage the various directions in the script apply. (Up Centre, Down Left, etc. See Figure 2.) It will be seen that "right" is the actor's right, not the audience's. Other terms such as Prompt Side and Opposite Prompt may be met with, the former indicating the left, the latter, the right, but in practice the prompter may be either side. The terms are not reliable, and lead to possible confusion. (The prompter will take a position as directed by the S.M.)

Other pages in the script can be used for notes of curtain music, incidental music (with its duration), the running-time of each scene, the allocation of jobs to stage helpers, an estimate of the time needed for scene-changing (upon which the length of the intervals may depend), etc., while on the "working" pages in the body of the script can be noted opposite the appropriate cues the lighting effects (in green), sound effects (in red), and general notes of changes of scenery, etc. (in blue), using ink for a clear reference and permanent record. (See Figure 1.)

Finally, a "thumb" index will facilitate quick reference to the notes and scenes. Loose-leaf ledger tabs can be used, or gummed tabs stuck at the tops (or sides) of the pages.

The above preparations can all be made before rehearsals start. We deal with the use of the script at rehearsals and productions in later chapters.

Surveying the Stage

The ground plans mentioned above are not to scale. They are only diagrams that indicate positions. For designing his set the S.M. will need to make a larger drawing to scale. He should, therefore, visit the hall to inspect the stage, to make his survey, and, while on the spot, sum up the general facilities that are available.

Stages vary enormously. For purposes of illustration we will assume a stage of some 30 ft. by 15 ft., high enough to take

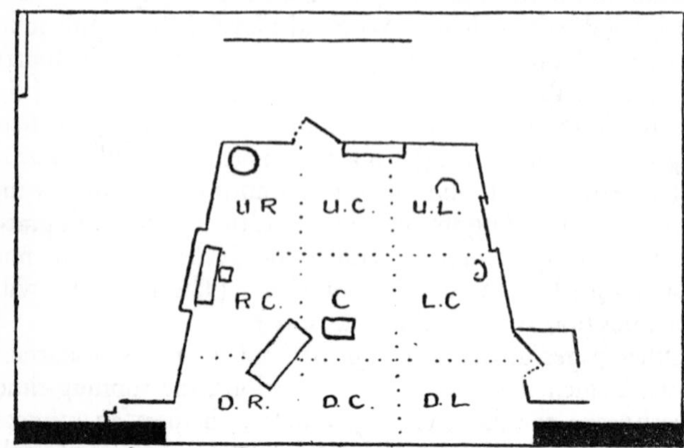

Fig. 2: Ground Plan of a Typical Set showing various positions on stage. (For Prompt Copy).

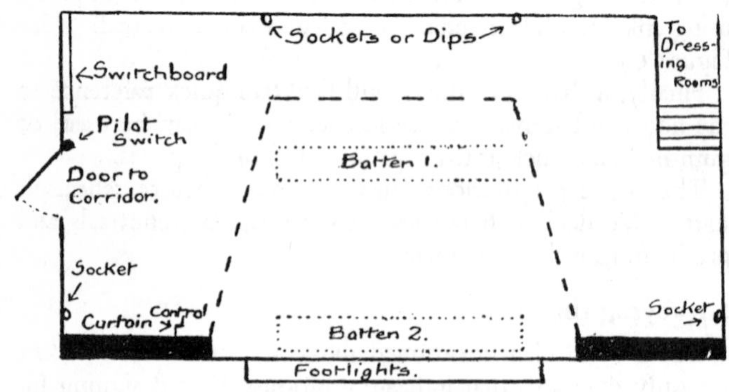

Fig. 3: Typical Ground Plan of Small Stage
Dotted line – Batten Lights.
Broken line – Acting Area.

scenery 10 ft. high. These are overall measurements, covering the entire stage. The considerably smaller area left after erecting scenery is known as the "acting area." (See Chapter III.) An assistant at the survey is desirable. For those who are unused to making plans, we mention that the first step is to draw roughly the shape of the stage as it would appear to an observer above it. (See Figure 3.) The positions of stairs, doors, lights, etc., are shown. Accurate measurements, as below, are then made, the final scale drawing being prepared at home, preferably on graph paper ruled in $\frac{1}{12}$-in. squares, a scale of $\frac{1}{2}$ in. to the foot being used. (Graph paper ruled in $\frac{1}{10}$-in. squares is not so convenient when working in feet and inches.) It will be necessary to measure the depth of the stage (i.e. the distance from footlights to rear of stage) the width (from wall to wall), the distance between the front curtains when opened, the approximate size of the acting area (making due allowance for the footlights should they be covered at the time of the survey), and the position of the overhead battens (i.e. the permanent lights arranged in one or more rows over the stage). When planning visibility (lines of sight) it is also useful to know the position of the extreme ends of the front row of seats used by the audience.

Measurements of the elevation (the stage as seen from the front) may also be useful. Accurate measuring will call for step-ladders, but estimates may have to suffice. They should include the height from floor of stage to top of proscenium arch (i.e. the "frame" through which the audience sees the play), and the height to the curtain rail. The height of the battens, cross-beams, and top-of-stage fittings generally (sometimes known as "the grid") may also be required. The grid is often masked by one or more "borders." It should be ascertained if these are adjustable or permanently fixed.

Before leaving the hall, the S.M. should check, and note, the following: Location of switchboard, dips and sockets (i.e. electricity points), and the position the switchboard operator will be in when operating the lights; the location of the switches controlling the house (audience) lights; the possibility of a separate socket and switch for an amplifier; (if linked with the general lighting, the amplifier may cease to work if lights are turned off during the play). Some halls are fitted with dimmers, i.e. sliding switches capable of graduating lights from full brightness to zero. The S.M. should find out with what points and sockets these are connected. Stage lighting is dealt with in a volume specially written for this Series, but the S.M. will need to know the above details when planning his production.

The type of front curtains and their control should be noted. They are likely to be one of two types. "Tableau," or "festooned," curtains are drawn up and to the side, permitting a quick curtain. "Draw" or "trailing" curtains slide along a rail and are slower in operation. Either type may be controlled by a drum and handle, or by ropes. To avoid confusion "on the night" (see Chapter VII) it is essential to know exactly how to handle these controls.

Unusual structural features, such as pillars on the stage, low roof beams, etc., which are likely to interfere with scenery, should be observed. Some stages have a rake, i.e. a slight slope from the back down to the footlights. This slope can be ignored, as any slight trouble it gives when the set is being erected can be put right (see Chapter VII). The S.M. may also meet with the sprung stage. This calls for no special consideration, except that he can be assured that the alarming squeaks caused by walking on the empty stage will disappear when the scenery and furniture are in place.

Existing scenery, back-cloths, rostra or steps that are often lying about the hall, may prove useful and, if required, permission to use them should be sought: it is not safe to assume that they will still be about when the society puts on its play.

If the particular production is insured, the insurance company may require the society to nominate a fireman—usually he is the S.M. The fire-fighting appliances should, therefore, be located, and noted on the plan. These must always be accessible and unobstructed.

Dressing-room accommodation should also be inspected.

To comply with legal regulations in some localities separate accommodations for men and women should be available. If only one room is available, this can be curtained.

Finally, on leaving, the S.M. will ascertain the best point for unloading his scenery.

Good relations with the caretaker of the school or hall are essential. The S.M. is very much in his hands, and, although he will wish to consult him on several points, the caretaker's time and other commitments should be respected. The society's treasurer may have cause to regard the "Gratuity to Caretaker" as a worthwhile expense.

CHAPTER III

DESIGNING AND MAKING THE SET

Designing the Set

THE S.M. is now ready to design his set. He can base his ideas on the photograph sometimes shown in the text; he can be guided by the description set out in the play; he will certainly also need to use his imagination.

His main task, as designer, is to give the audience something pleasing to the eye and suitable to the action and atmosphere of the play, yet allowing the cast and stage staff to move with a minimum of trouble. Being also the stage manager, he will, by now, have a good knowledge of the play.

No hard and fast rules can be laid down, owing to the variety of stages and plays, but, first, the approximate acting area should be marked on the ground plan with dotted lines (see Figure 3), and on these lines should be shown the position of the doors, windows, stairs, fireplace, etc. He can then better judge how much space he will have for his furniture: when this is in position it is often surprising how little space there is left—hence the emphasis (in Chapter II) on essentials. It may be necessary to adjust the set to accommodate the furniture, e.g. to make a recess to take a couch or table. It should be remembered that the more physical action in the play, the more space is required for acting; in a "wordy" play, more space can be taken up by furniture, but if the play features duels, fights, crowd scenes, dancing, etc., cramping should be avoided. Costumes should be borne in mind; one player in a crinoline can take up the room of two people in modern dress.

The easiest design is the straightforward three-walled set (back and two sides), but alcoves and angles can be introduced to make the scene more interesting. The set is often "splayed" (see Figure 2), i.e. it tapers slightly towards the back. This aids visibility (as the line of sight from the extreme ends of the front row of the audience will readily show). The maximum use should be made of a stage, remembering that depth (from the back of the stage to the footlights) is as valuable to a producer as width. Sometimes, for example, a door UC is required on a very shallow stage. The whole set need not be brought forward to allow this door to open, for the door can be set at an angle. (See Figure 4.) Unless essential to some incident in the play, doors should open outwards, into the wings; they should be hung with the hinges up-stage in order to allow more room for exits and entrances, and the backing is less visible. (See Figure 5.) Doors should be sited according to the producer's wishes and the demands of the text; the position of a window is less important and can usually be at variance with the text without unduly upsetting the moves of the play. All openings have to be "backed" with a painted flat or a draped curtain (see Figures 4 and 5) so that an audience, looking through the window or door, will see something appropriate to the scene, e.g. the wall of the next room, a blue sky, trees, etc. The lighting of these backings should not be overlooked. (See Chapter 5.)

A little research into styles of architecture may be necessary to get the correct effect of period. Photographic accuracy is not essential, but an audience will usually notice glaring anachronisms. Most periods of history have their distinctive features of ornament and decoration, and a restrained use of these motifs will suggest the period adequately. There are useful and detailed books on this subject. (See Chapter IX.) Obviously the type of set should fit the style of the play and its production. A play written in verse or "elevated prose" will call for a dignified background; elegant dialogue of the Restoration period requires its elegant furniture and interior; the robust vigour of Elizabethan comedy would ill-accord with flimsy chairs and tables and delicate curtains.

The value of differing acting levels is often overlooked. The

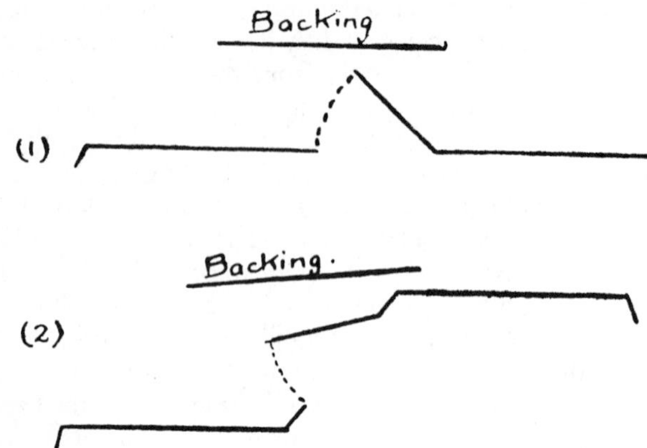

Fig. 4: Showing how an angled setting of a door can afford extra playing area.
(1) Door set parallel.
(2) Door set at angle.

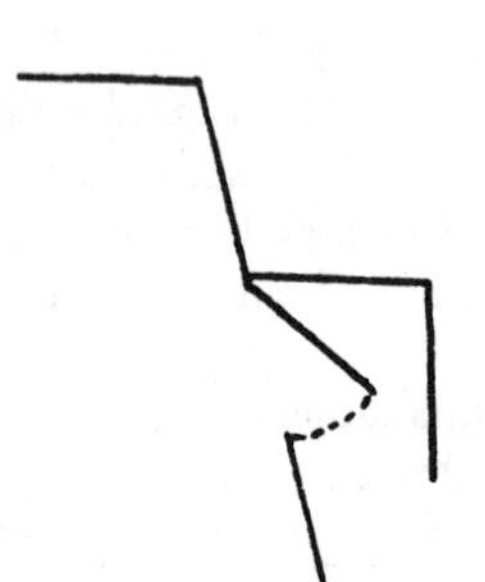

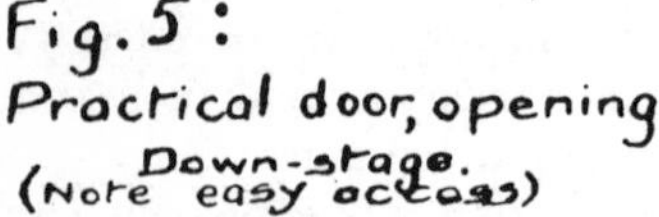

Fig. 5:
Practical door, opening Down-stage. (Note easy access)

Impractical door opening Up-stage (difficult access).

grouping and "patterning" of the characters is the producer's job, but the S.M. may need to remind him of the use of rostra, i.e. platforms of various sizes. For example, double french windows can be recessed back from the wall of the set and raised one or two steps from floor level; if placed UC, the producer will have a fine central focusing point for important entrances. Almost any entrance can be treated similarly; the Greek or Roman setting can have its temple steps, the medieval play its heavy wooden staircase; the modern country house its terrace raised above the level of the lounge; the slum kitchen or sordid café can be set as a basement with steps leading into it from the outside. (See Fig. 26.) In fantasy, realism can be abandoned and decorative effect be the criterion. Stairs can give a variety of acting heights, but, when planning, the S.M. should know the height of his tallest actor who will use them so that he can make sure the character will be completely visible and not appear to be decapitated to the gallery or back rows of the audience. Complete staircases need seldom be shown. After two or three stairs a platform should be used to represent a landing, giving the impression that a character arriving there is about to ascend a further flight.

In Figure 6 we have shown, as specimens, three different designs, all of which were executed in the same basic fibre-boarded flats: (A) represents the lounge and living room in *You Can't Take it With You* (Kaufman). A cast of nineteen had to use this room; therefore as much acting space as possible was required. The two doors were essential, together with the curtained archway, with the stairs being visible behind. (B) represents the small Irish cottage of *Riders to the Sea* (Synge), important features of which were a peat loft DR and stable door, UC. The door had to be sufficiently down (forward) to allow a stretcher to come through it and the loft had to be reached by a small pair of steps. The acting area could be cut down as the cast was small. In (C) it was again possible to cut down on the acting area as the play, *The Heiress* (Goetz), called for little physical action. The diagram shows the front parlour and hallway of a large Victorian house. Both hall and

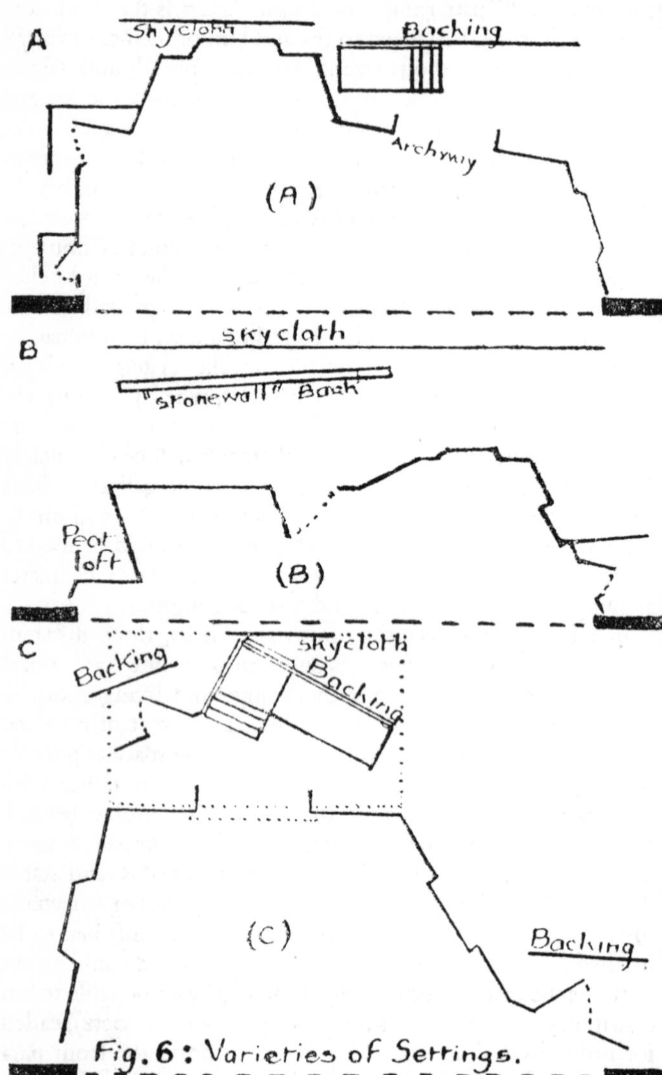

Fig. 6: Varieties of Settings.

parlour were important, and the angle of the stairs allowed the players to avoid presenting their profiles when entering or leaving by them. The whole hallway and stairs were mounted on a 9-in. rostrum (shown by a dotted line in the figure) which descended by a 4½-in. step into the room. The archway was curtained and the stair window was set at the top of the flat, giving an illusion of height.

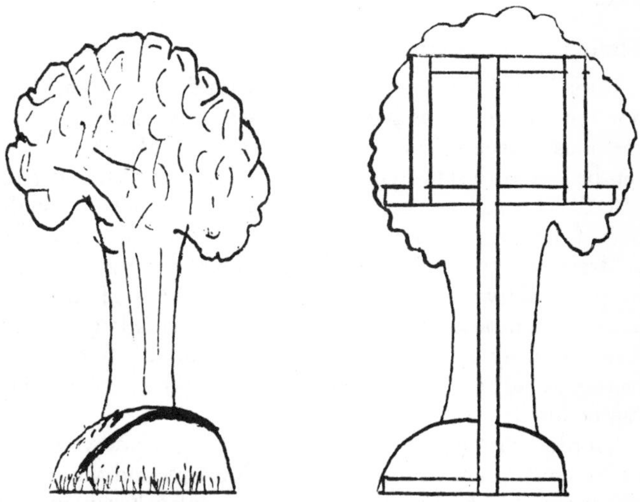

Fig. 7: Tree Cut-out. Front and Back:

Exterior Sets

These are usually represented by curtain backcloths and cut-outs. A cut-out is an outline (hedge, trees, end of a house, rock, etc.) made of hardboard or plywood cut out to the required shape and mounted on a frame. (Figure 7.) At best these are convincing symbols, and care should be taken to keep the play artistically homogeneous. For example, a convincing interior scene, complete with every realistic detail, should not be followed by symbolical trees and pretty, but artificial, shrubs in pots, etc. With a play that calls for several very different scenes it is best to rely on suggestion throughout. (A good exercise in this technique is afforded by Dodie Smith's comedy, *Call it a Day*, which demands two bedrooms, a solicitor's office, a kitchen, a garden, and an artist's studio!)

The painted representation of small properties such as books, vases, pictures, clock is not recommended. They do not look convincing in the average hall. The real things should be used.

Scene Changing with the "Box" Set

If the "box" set is used for a play with different scenes, and not the curtain set as suggested above, three main practical methods of scene-changing are open to the S.M. A small set can be erected inside a larger, and removed (perhaps later replaced) to reveal a second scene (it may be possible to use the flats of the outer set as backings for the inner one). Secondly, a "traverse" curtain can be used. This is a curtain that can be quickly drawn across the stage halving its depth and allowing a scene to proceed in front of it, while behind it the next scene is being prepared. Traverse curtains do not usually feature as part of the equipment of halls and schools. They can be hired.

Thirdly, changes can be made by altering window designs, or by converting a fireplace into a doorway and vice versa. As an example of this we have taken the play *Bonaventure* by Charlotte Hastings. This was performed by the authors' own dramatic group. It called for two main scenes: first, the Great Hall of a convent; secondly, the private room of one of the nursing sisters. The set (see Figure 8) was designed with both these scenes in mind and constructed with fibre-board (as described later in this chapter). These two scenes were represented by flats painted to represent stone slabs. In the Great Hall scene DL was a door flat (*a*) hung with a fireplace cowling and inserted with a "hearth stone" made of fibre-boarding. This formed the fireplace. Up-stage of this was a 1-foot flat (*b*) hinged to (*a*). Next to this was an exit backed by a movable flat (*d*). (*c*) represents stairs and rostrum leading behind

Fig. 8:

(e)
(f)
(c)
(d)
(b)
(g)
(a)
"Bonaventure":
The Great Hall.

"Bonaventure":
Sister Mary's room.

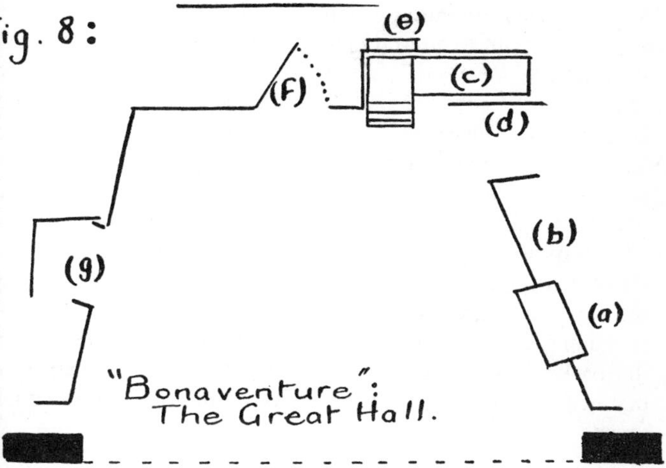

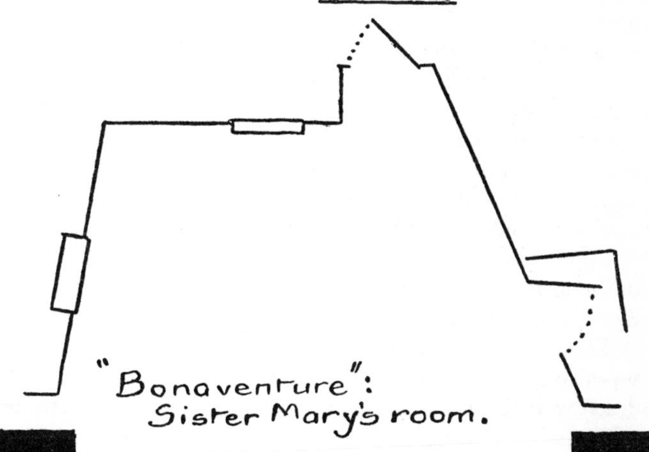

(*d*) into the wings. Behind the stairs (*c*) was a door flat (*e*) with a lattice window hung in the opening. UC was a door (*f*) opening out to a terrace and backed with a sky backcloth. RC was a "revealed" (see below) archway (*g*) apparently leading to the entrance hall. To change the scene from the Hall to the private room the stairs and rostrum (*c*) were "struck" (removed), (*d*) was swivelled to meet (*b*), which was swung round to follow the line of (*a*) and to meet the back wall flats. The window (*e*) was taken from the doorway and a backing put into place. The cowling from (*a*) was hung on the door (*f*) and a stove and back-cloth were inserted, leaving the doorway and backing at (*a*). A window seat was inserted in the arch (*g*) with the window frame from (*e*) hung on the back. The scene was thus completely transformed in a matter of minutes, and restored to its original form with equal speed.

Constructing the Set

When designing and making the set, the S.M. will be working with units of scenery known as "flats." He may have to work with existing scenery owned by his society, or he may have to construct his own. Flats are usually made 10 ft. or 12 ft. high with widths varying between 4 ft. and 1 ft. (Wide flats can always be reduced, for scenery effects, by overlapping or setting at an angle.) Few halls will take scenery of over 10 ft. high, but should an unusually lofty stage be met with, the S.M. can easily extend his flats in the manner explained below.

When a set is constructed, future productions should be borne in mind, hence the range of adaptable flats is suggested. These can be interchanged and re-decorated for future plays.

Traditionally, flats are made of canvas stretched over a wooden frame. They are in common use, and we, therefore, describe their construction while suggesting below cheaper substitutes.

To make a canvas flat 10 ft. by 4 ft., two lengths of timber of 10 ft. and four of 4 ft. are required. Four triangular plywood corner plates, about 6 ins. by 6 ins. by 9 ins., will be required for strengthening. Timber should be $\frac{5}{8}$–$\frac{7}{8}$ in. thick by 2–2½ ins. wide, and planed smooth. The frame of 10 ft. by 4 ft. is made, using the half-check or half-joint. (See Figure 9.) The remaining two short lengths are similarly jointed and fitted at a third from each end of the frame, the uprights being recessed to take them. All joints should be screwed, and not glued. Finally, the corner pieces are screwed in place, making sure that the angles are right angles. (See Figure 10.) Over this frame is stretched the canvas, which is nailed and, preferably, glued (on the sides, not the face, of the frame). Larger flats will need wider timber and more strutting.

Canvas, burlap, and well-seasoned timber necessary for the above are expensive. An alternative is to use fibre insulating board about ¼ in. thick and made in sheets of 8 ft. by 4 ft. It is light in weight, with a surface, when primed, amenable to paint or distemper. Also it is not prone to flap as is canvas. It is framed on the lines of the canvas flats, but cheap, unplaned wood can be used. (See Figure 11.) The boards should be nailed to the wooden frame with large-headed clout nails.

Both types of flat will need tie-off lines and cleats for erection purposes, and ordinary sash or linen lines, obtainable from the ironmonger in 12-yard lengths, can be used. The cleats should be fixed some 2 ft. from the top of the flat at the back. Here holes, large enough to take the rope, are drilled diagonally from the inside edge of the left-hand rail through to the back of the frame. The line, which should be about 8 ft. long, is threaded through and knotted on the inside. With cheap or small timber a screw-eye can be used instead of the drilled hole. (See Figures 10 and 11.) Opposite, on the right-hand rail, a cleat is fixed. A cleat resembles the ordinary domestic "tie-off" plate used for clothes lines, etc. (See Figure 10.) Such cleats can be bought, or they can be made cheaply by recessing rough wood. (See Figure 11.) Finally, two tie-off round-headed screws are fixed 2 ft. from the bottom on both the upright rails. (See Figures 10 and 11.) The method of lashing is shown in Figure 12 and described in Chapter VII.

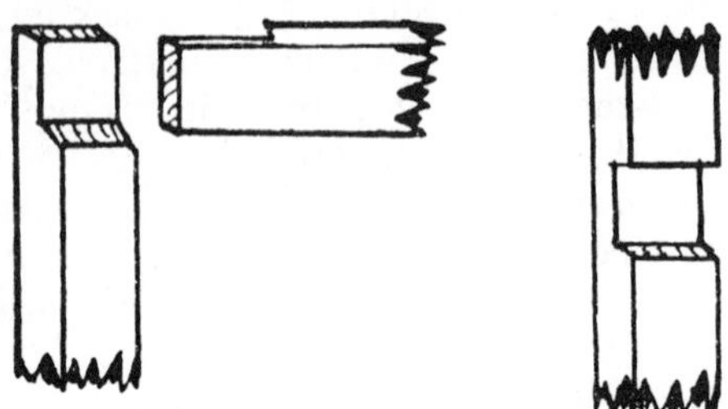

Fig. 9: Half-joint and Recessed Half-joint.

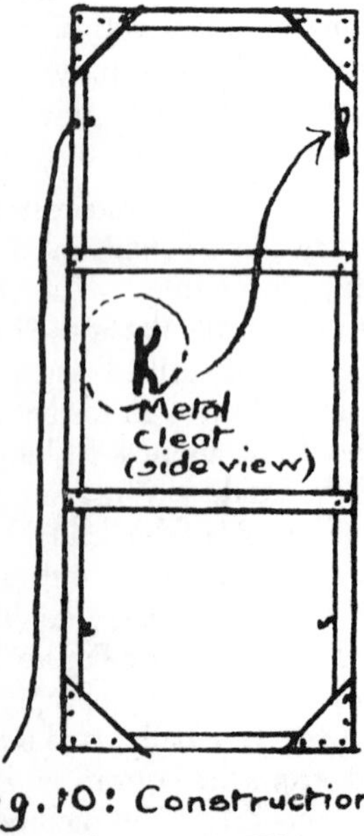

Tie-off line

Metal cleat (side view)

Wooden cleat (side view)

Tie-off screws

Fig. 10: Construction of Canvas Flat.

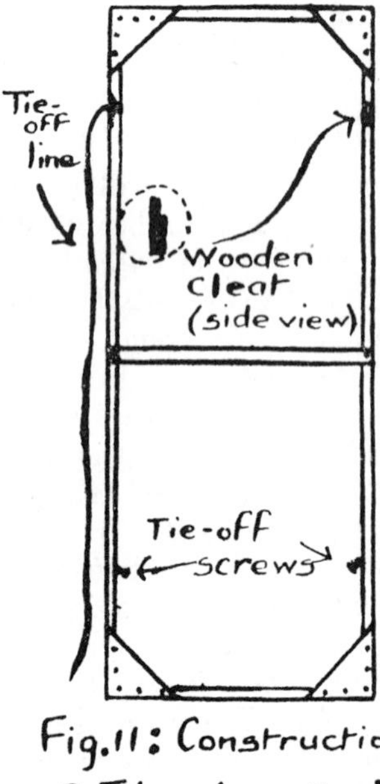

Fig. 11: Construction of Fibre-boarding Flat

To erect the flats (see Chapter VII) braces are also required. Extending braces are obtainable but are expensive; they are fitted at the top with "horns," which hook into screw-eyes inserted into the rails of the flat, the bottom of the brace being fitted with a metal plate for fixing to the floor of the stage. A cheap substitute can be made with a length of wood 1 in. by 1 in., 6 ft. long, using angle-plates top and bottom. If wide plates are available, two flats can be braced with one brace (see Figure 13) but the S.M. may find it easier to use ordinary shelf brackets opened out to the required angle.

If flats are to be stored in confined spaces, it may be desirable to make them to fold; a 10-ft. flat would thus be made of two sections (6 ft. and 4 ft.), hinged at the back and with two holes drilled near the hinges through the two end rails. Through these holes metal pegs or taper pins are inserted and these hold the two sections firmly in place. (See Figure 14.) The pins are best drilled and attached with string to the frame of the flat so that they are not easily lost. This folding method can be used if it is desired to extend existing flats say from 10 ft. to 12 ft. or 14 ft. high.

Doors, Windows, and Fireplaces

These should be built into complete flats with reveals, if desired. A reveal is the timber or boarding set at right angles to the flat (and hinged to facilitate storage) to give the impression of thickness of a door frame or wall. (See Figure 15.) Such flats are built as above. It should be remembered that the opening must be framed, using the recess and half-joint. For doors and french windows where the opening extends to the floor, sill irons are necessary. These are strips of rigid metal that can be covered with carpet, if desired, though being at floor level they are not conspicuous. Angled strips can be used, or one strip the width of the flat achieves the same purpose. (See Figure 16.) If larger timber, as in the rest of the flat, is used across the opening, the cast are likely to trip. Unless he is an expert the S.M. should not attempt to fit the doors exactly, but should make the door about an inch

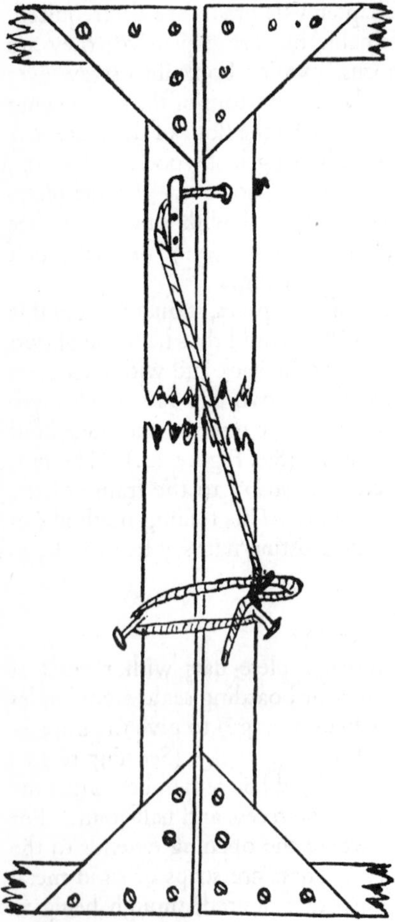

Fig. 12: Method of lashing Flats.

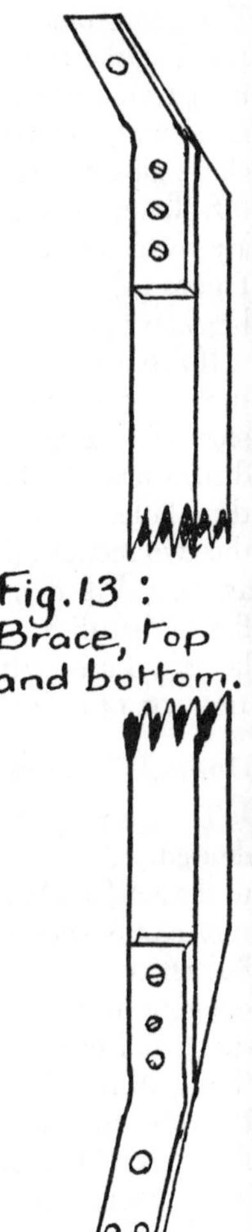

Fig. 13: Brace, top and bottom.

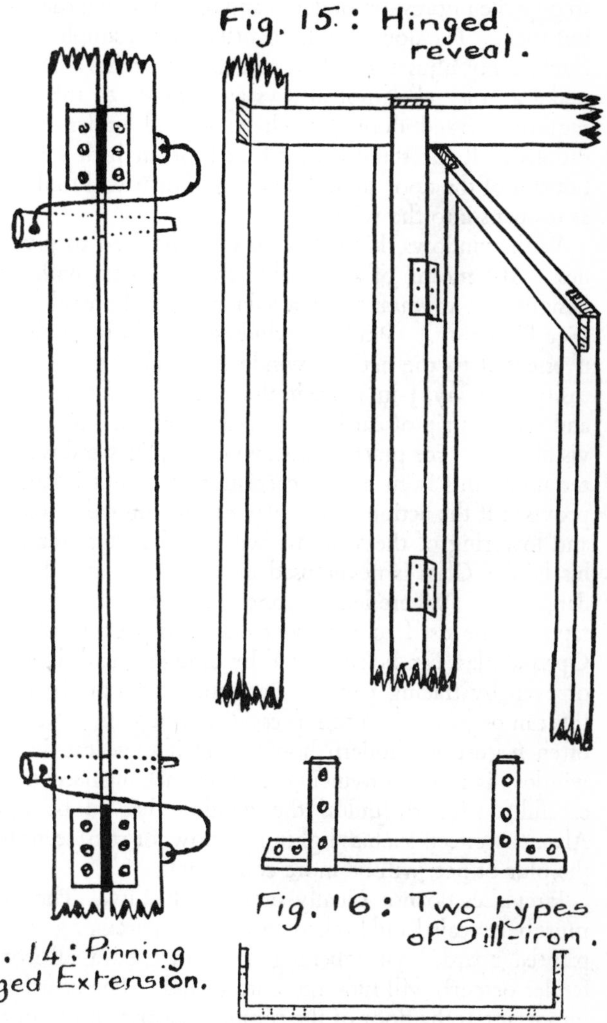

Fig. 15: Hinged reveal.

Fig. 16: Two types of Sill-iron.

Fig. 14: Pinning a hinged Extension.

oversize so that the edge comes to rest against the door frame to give the impression of depth and to ensure that the door will not stick. The door should be fitted with a simple spring clip catch, easily adjustable. Ball-and-socket catches are expensive, make a noisy click not always appropriate to the play, and require a fitted door (which may foul under stage conditions). If the stage is raked, at least an inch space at the bottom of the door should be allowed or it will foul the floor as it opens into the wings.

With windows, hinged reveals can be used to give thickness. By means of detachable frames fitted with varying designs the appearance of a window can be easily changed (See Figure 17.) Practical windows should be avoided, but, if essential to the action, windows should be made to open easily with, say, ½-in. space in the middle (for lattice windows) and with a strip of card or ply tacked on one side to hide the visible gap. For practical sash windows, lines and weights are required; this is an expert carpenter's job, but it can be improvised if the action of the play can be limited to the raising and lowering of the window without the character releasing his hold. Glass is never used in windows. It is heavy and dangerous. Where leaded panes have to be suggested, black tape can be used to represent diamond-pane windows, etc. Opaque glass can be suggested by draughtsman's linen paper, or even by tracing paper if permanence is not essential, and this can be painted on to represent stained glass. Net curtains often feature in modern houses, and if these can be used, a window is more convincing, and its backing need not be so carefully painted (unless the window has to be opened). Also, any effects such as lightning, snow, or rain, seen through the blur of net, will be more convincing.

Fireplaces do not usually present difficulty. The opening must be revealed and backed, using black curtaining or a black-painted board. The opening does not need a sill iron, as a fender or curb will hide the bottom rail. The hearthstone is important as the floor of the room, or carpet, must not appear to go up to the grate itself; it can be made of an oblong sheet

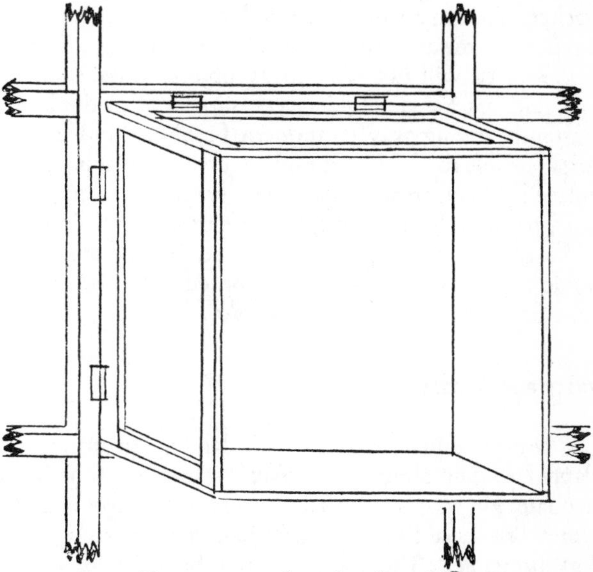

Fig. 17: Revealed Window Opening.

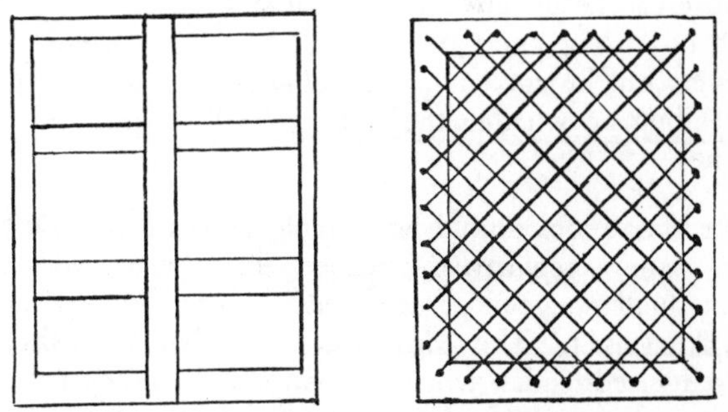

Two types of Frames which could be fitted to the above.

of fibre-boarding. The mantel-shelf is fitted with angle brackets, and ornamented surrounds can be painted or modelled in relief my means of papier mâché (see Chapter IV). The mantel-piece will not take heavy objects unless it is heavily built and bracketed. Older-type surrounds in the home are constantly giving way to modern fireplaces, and it is sometimes possible to obtain a complete surround that has thus been replaced. Such an acquisition has everything to commend it, apart, perhaps, from its weight. Fenders or curbs can usually be borrowed; a fender can easily be made from plywood, moulding, and broomsticks, and painted. The actual effect of a live fire is dealt with in Chapter V.

Stairs and Rostra

A complete unit of stairs with landing (rostrum) can be adapted to suit almost any play. Three or four steps are adequate for most sets. They must not be too large. The framework should be of 2 in. by 2 in. timber, using the half-joint principle. The treads should be covered with $\frac{5}{8}$-in. boarding of the type used for packing cases. The risers (upright faces) can be filled in with any material. (See Figure 18.) The rostrum can be in the form of a table with short legs, but it must be strong enough to hold about five people. Stair banisters can be cut out of boarding or 1-in. square timber (depending on whether the audience will see more than the outline).

The above jobs should be possible with a few basic tools, (saw, plane, screwdriver, hammer, chisel, rule, and square) with a small garage or garden shed as a workshop. A nest of saws is an asset. This consists of a saw handle with three different-sized blades, which can cut curves and corners (and which can be obtained at Woolworth's Stores). A tommy-bar and punch may be required when erecting the set. (See Figure 20 and Chapter VII.)

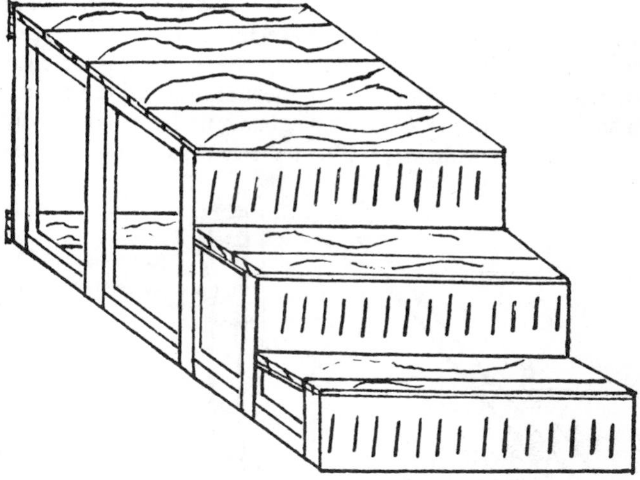

Fig. 18: Stairs made from packing cases using frame of 2"×2" timber and Half-joints.

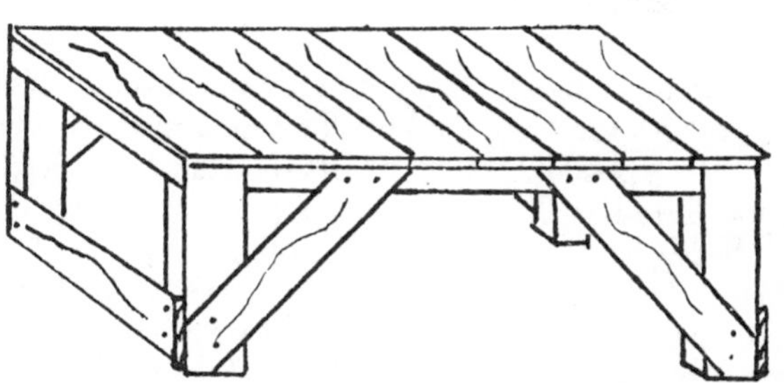

Fig. 19: Rostrum made from packing case timber.

Painting

Scene painting is simply an exaggerated form of drawing and colouring where boldness of execution is more important than detail. The natural tendency, when working at close quarters, is to give undue finish to the work that will be wasted under stage lighting. On the other hand, undue exaggeration, such as is met with in professional scene painting, is to be

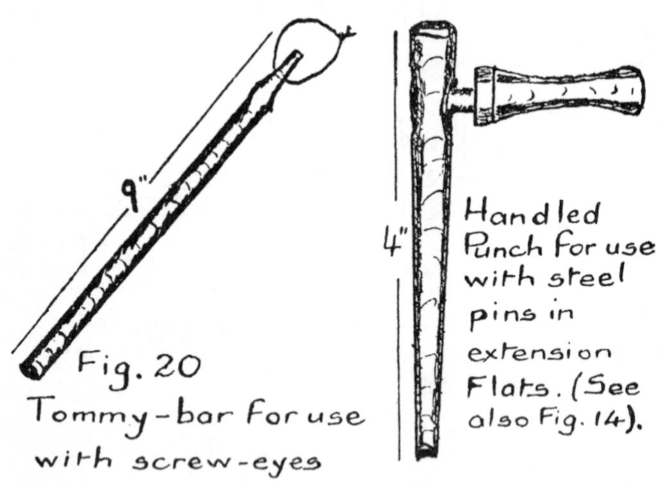

avoided, for the powerful lighting and long-distance vision that call for this technique will not be found in the amateur theatre. It is advisable to test colours by painting a piece of canvas or fibre-boarding and allowing the paint to dry; colours always dry lighter. The effect of coloured stage lights on a scene is dealt with in Stage Lighting in this Series, but the S.M. can keep a check on his effects by throwing various colours on his work (this can be done by shining a high-powered electric lead light through coloured gelatine). Colour effects should never be judged by daylight.

Before painting, the S.M. should prime his flats with glue size, which should be left to dry. If not too expensive, stage water-colour paints should be used; distemper, mixed with size, however, is satisfactory, and will not rub off, but the range of colours is not wide. Colour mixing should be experimented with: for example, red and blue in paint produce purple, but in distemper a dove grey will be the result. Glossy paints should not be used, as glaze, under stage lighting, destroys the appearance of colour.

Modern wallpaper effects can be obtained by "stippling"; the flat is painted with a basic colour, then dabbed over with a sponge dipped in another colour, the mixture of which should be fairly thick to avoid running. Two or more colours can be used in this way. For more definite patterns stencils cut from card or gelatine should be used. It is convenient to lay the flat face-upwards on the floor and to work with a short-bristled brush. To get the effect of a slightly dirty, well-lived in room a colour slightly darker than the basic colour of the wall should be stippled. Over a fireplace the dirt will be at the top of the wall, but near the doors, or where chair-backs rub, there will be grime at shoulder height. The soiled area near the handle on a light-coloured door should not be overlooked in this type of room. When panels, ledges, or mouldings are being painted on doors or flats the shadows should be away from the apparent source of light (window, electric light, etc.).

Doors and woodwork can be painted to simulate a stained and polished finish with the grain showing through. The surface should be given a coat of terra-cotta distemper fairly thick, and allowed to dry. Ordinary water stain should then be applied, and, when this is still wet, drawn up and down (if this is to be the direction of the grain) with a graining comb and allowed to dry. Some of the lines can be picked out in black with a thin lining brush, if desired. The effect will be polished and grained wood which will not, however, reflect light (which must be avoided). Water stain can be obtained in crystal form, known as Vandyke Crystals, and should be watered down to the required colour. Graining combs made of rubber can be bought. An ordinary hair comb cut to about half its width with some of the teeth removed will give an uneven graining, but it needs a light touch. Stiff card, suitably notched, will also serve for a short time, but it quickly becomes soggy.

A paint-spraying gun will simplify large-scale painting, but it is expensive. A small type, used with a domestic vacuum cleaner, is relatively cheap, but the container requires constant re-filling; it can be used for shading or "dirtying down" effects.

Having built and decorated his set, the S.M. must fireproof it. There are several formulae laid down. A good working preparation is: phosphate of ammonia, 1 lb.; sal ammoniac, 2 lb.; water, 1½ gallons. The proofing should be done only a short time before the production. The solution can be applied with a brush, or sprayed on to the backs of the flats, care being taken that the liquid does not reach the colours on the front of the flat.

If the S.M .is in any doubt about fire precautions generally, it is best to contact the local fire department.

The large scenic back-cloth is not likely to feature in the average amateur production, but the S.M. may be called on to produce one for purposes of a pantomime or children's play. Also some of the larger backings of landscapes, etc., seen through up-stage windows may be regarded as miniature scenic back-cloths. It will usually be necessary to paint a large canvas at the hall itself, as this cannot be done satisfactorily in the garage or small studio. If the cloth is suspended in position against the back of the stage, the S.M. can work direct; otherwise it becomes necessary to lay the cloth on the floor and to walk on it, taking care not to step on any part that is wet.

Flats, butted together edge to edge, can be used to make one large scene for these purposes. They can be painted separately and assembled on the stage, but it is difficult to disguise the joins.

Whichever method is used, the S.M. is likely to be working from a small picture or design. To transfer this to the large area the picture is squared off. The canvas or assembled flats are similarly treated, using a convenient scale. For short lines a straight-edge and charcoal can be used. For long lines a "snap line" is quicker. This consists of a length of string rubbed with charcoal. It is fastened at one end of the area, drawn taut over the proposed line, and plucked. As it strikes the surface a black line results. The artist then draws his scene in charcoal and follows his "squared-off" sketch. If this preliminary sketch is drawn competently, the scene-painter can reproduce the effect on a large scale, even though he may have no drawing skill.

Curtain Sets

Amateurs sometimes "work in curtains," i.e. use curtains instead of scenery flats, though the use of fireplace flats, etc., can be incorporated. This is a feature of drama festivals and is dealt with in Chapter VIII. Should the S.M. be responsible for the initial installation of this type of curtain for his society, he should consider Bolton sheeting of a neutral shade. Size, method of hanging, etc., will depend upon the hall to be used. The S.M. may be responsible also for the curtain fittings, in which case the domestic type of curtain runner is satisfactory, as it can be shaped easily to form the required surround. The fixing of curtain runners is usually done by the firm supplying the materials. It is specialized work, but the S.M. may be called in to advise on the layout. This should be carefully considered, as, unlike flats, the acting area and basic shape of the set will be permanent when the fittings are in place. Curtains should be in several separate sections to allow for all possible variations of exits, entrances, and the insertion of flats, etc. Usually such curtains are fireproofed by the manufacturers.

Figure 21 shows three possible lay-outs, using curtains. (A) is a common design, but all exits in the back drapes have to be backed. Furniture placed at the sides of this type of setting should follow the line of the splay. Figure (B) shows another design, usually met with at festivals. As in the other plans in this figure, the curtains are shown as a continuous line,

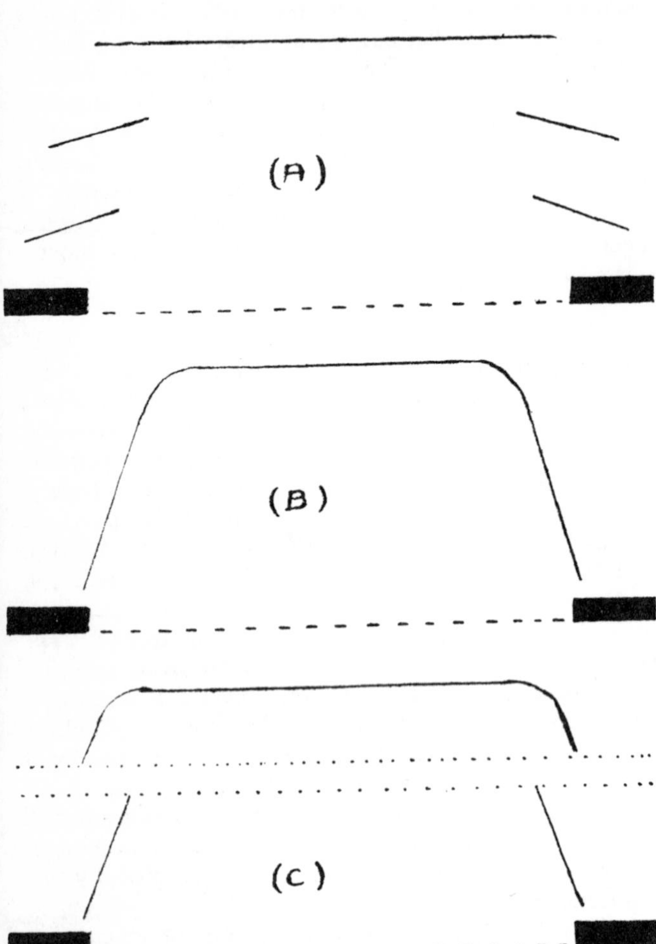

Fig. 21: The curtain set: Three arrangements. (initial installation).

but they are made up of narrower sections, and here all access "gaps," back or side, will need to be backed. Figure (c) demonstrates how special features found in various halls may be used. The double dotted line represents a beam, about 18 ins. in depth, which prevented the curtain runner from forming a continuous line. The stage formed part of a new school, and it was not desirable to disfigure the ceiling with a heavy wooden frame lowered to the height of the beam. The line of the curtain rail was, therefore, broken as shown. This enabled it to be battened against the ceiling, and also gave two access gaps that could be used without backing.

The Model

A model of the stage and set is not only interesting in itself, but also of help to the producer and cast who do not always find it easy to visualize the scene as it will appear finally. Some S.Ms. prefer to make a model first and to use it as a basis for their design; others work out their set on paper and construct a model, if at all, later. Also some producers like to demonstrate their production moves on a model, using counters to represent the characters.

Cartridge paper or ordinary "shoe-box" cardboard can be used. A base will be required (wood, thick card, or an inverted cardboard lid) which need not show the height of the stage from floor level, unless desired. On this base should be indicated the ground plan, which can be reproduced by using carbon paper face down, the plan already made by the S.M. in his stage survey being used, and the design being traced through. Cardboard rectangles for flats can then be made to represent the scene with whatever accuracy or detail the S.M. chooses. Furniture and stage properties need be shown in outline only, for unless the model is on a large scale the making of miniature tables and chairs, etc., is a finicky business.

CHAPTER IV

FURNITURE AND PROPERTIES

THE type of furniture used in the play depends largely upon the play itself and also upon the producer, who should not be biased appreciably by the designer. For most modern settings, it is usually more convenient to borrow, either from a local furniture dealer or from members of the society and their friends. A free advertisement in the programme often satisfies the lending firm; otherwise the society may find that hiring is rather expensive. The advantage of personal loan is that members of the cast can often make themselves familiar with the furniture well before the performance; they may even be able to rehearse with it. Also, as most amateurs are working people, it is easier to arrange collection, etc., out of working hours.

The size of furniture should be considered carefully; it is better to err on the small side rather than on the large, thus avoiding filling up too much valuable acting space.

The modern scene often features the hard-worked settee and easy chairs. The very deep type may give actresses trouble with their skirts. They may be difficult to rise from; and, usually, they are cumbersome to move about. Therefore, get small, light-weight suites, if possible. Avoid placing a settee full-on to the audience in which position it may give the appearance of a posed photograph when it seats more than two characters. Provided the cast have good carrying voices, it is possible to have the settee backing the audience and facing the fireplace, as most settees do, instead of being isolated in the centre of a room and facing the imaginary "fourth wall." If drawers in sideboards, etc., are to be used, make sure that they operate easily and do not stick (wax polish or soap rubbed on the points of friction helps). Highly-polished furniture is best avoided.

When period furniture has to be used, the S.M. should acquaint himself with the general style that is appropriate to the era. If necessary, reference books should be consulted. As with stage design, absolute accuracy is not necessary, but the style should suggest the atmosphere of the period. All types of period furniture can be hired. Some styles can easily be made, using modern pieces as a basis and building up with fibre-boarding, ply, or papier mâché. Packing cases make a good basis for benches and couches, particularly those of the simple classical type. (See Figure 25, Chapter 8.) The audience has only a limited view of stage furniture—unless it is moved during or between scenes—and time need not be spent on refinements that won't be seen. Curtains and drapes can be used to disguise furniture; a large plush table-cloth, for example, can completely hide a modern table and make it correct for many different periods; the old-fashioned couch can be renovated with drapings carefully and artistically arranged; a piano stool similarly treated can be useful. Elegant furniture of the Restoration period is not easily home-made; it is safer to borrow or to hire it. New, reproduction furniture is not recommended as it usually has a high polish. The glass in china cabinets, etc., can be troublesome because of its high reflecting properties, but it can be treated satisfactorily. (See below.)

The society and the S.M. have a duty towards members and friends who lend furniture for use on the stage. Stages are often dirty, cramped places, and actors and the stage staff, under the stress of the production, may not use these properties with desirable care. The S.M. should warn his cast about possible damage, and keep a watchful eye on the property under his control.

A carpet often improves the appearance of a set and ensures quiet movement. It may even be essential. If used, it should, if possible, cover the whole acting area. Any curling edges should be lightly tacked down to avoid accidents. Small rugs on the stage can prove dangerous unless they are flat. If used, they should be placed in appropriate places, i.e. in front of the fireplace, at the foot of stairs, etc., and not merely used to fill up floor space. Large canvas floor coverings, known as "treads," are used in the professional theatre. Their purchase can be a good investment for a society with a hall of its own. The treads can be painted to represent lino, or carpeting, and are valuable in deadening the noise of feet. Failing a tread or carpet, the cast should be asked to wear soft shoes, where appropriate, as the clattering of hard footwear is distracting to an audience and destroys illusion.

Properties and Stage Dressings

Most modern, and many period, properties are easily borrowed. Many useful objects are to be found in people's attics and storerooms. Antique and junk shops are other sources of supply, but the S.M. will be wise not to burden himself with too much material that needs storing space. There are limits to the number of occasions on which properties can be used, for the society's followers will begin to recognize them! Antique, or unusual, properties, such as swords, goblets, sceptres, rings, fans, some ornaments, etc., can be hired from firms that specialize in these, but they can often be home-made. (See below.)

Pictures should have their glass removed and mirrors should be angled to avoid annoying the audience with reflections. In all properties and furniture that contain glass it is safer, however, to dull the surface by pasting it over with a sheet of thin grease-proof paper, or by rubbing it over with soap or whiting—though here the effect may be streaky.

Clocks

If clearly discernible, and an essential property, a clock must show time that is appropriate to the action of the play. It is possible to keep the clock "synchronized" with stage-time by extending the mechanism that operates the hands by introducing a shaft through the back of the clock, to be operated by a member of the stage-staff using a replica of the dial. This needs careful rehearsal and experiment. If the clock merely "dresses" the stage, its face should be kept angled away from the audience, or be stopped; the striking mechanism should certainly be silenced.

Ornaments

These should be used sparingly, unless an overcrowded Victorian effect is required. If not moved during the play, they should be wired to the mantel-piece with thin copper wire and drawing pins. Those that have to stand on tables, sideboards, etc., can be weighted with sand if there is any danger of their being knocked over. With vases, water is inadvisable and not usually necessary as real flowers should be avoided. Care should be taken to change flowers if the passing of time or season between scenes warrants it. Sometimes a bar or a shop scene has piles of dummy cartons stacked in pyramid form. Disused packets can be built up into stable units convenient for quick setting, and secured with Scotch tape. (See Fig. 26.)

Weapons

However realistic, real swords, even when blunt, are best left alone by amateurs, unless the weapon remains in its scabbard throughout the play. A sword should be worn early in rehearsals to avoid the possibility of a disastrous trip-up on the night. Shields can be made from ply or card, and decorated, if necessary, with papier mâché. Old-type guns made of wood and painted black can be convincing, but with pistols that have to be fired on-stage real weapons are necessary. The owner of a gun requires a fire-arms permit in many states and if the society buys its own the local police station should be asked about the permit. The noise of gunfire is dealt with in Chapter V.

Money

Stage money is obtainable, but usually notes and actual

coins can be used, unless the character has to handle very large quantites. Even here a large wad of paper money can be suggested by scrap paper cut to size and banded together to show real notes top and bottom.

Documents, etc.

Modern documents, i.e. telegrams, can be represented by the real thing. Envelopes that have to be opened on-stage should not be firmly sealed, only the tip of the flap should be fastened so that a player can open the envelope cleanly. Ancient documents and parchment can be suggested by painting thick white paper the correct shade (using clear varnish or Vandyke Crystals) or by using brown paper. Plasticine is useful for seals. Most S.M.s like to write the actual words on documents, letters, etc., but the actor should not rely on reading these. For periods before the Victorian age neither blotting paper nor steel-pointed pens should be used. Quills can be merely large feathers. Real ink is best kept off the stage.

Smoking

Fire precautions are necessary if smoking has to take place. Cigars should be cut. Matchboxes should have a couple of matches sticking out to avoid the player having to fumble; cigarette lighters are uncertain in real life. If one has to be used and it fails to work, the player should have matches and an appropriate remark ready. Some plays call for the knocking out of a pipe in the fireplace. If only unconvincing wooden noises are likely to be the result, this business is best omitted. Incidentally, modern acting editions often specify when a character must light up, stub out, or empty a pipe; often in practice this does not work out.

Portable Lights

Naked flame on the stage is dangerous; paraffin oil must not be used—hence such properties are best lighted electrically. (See Chapter V on Effects.)

Food and Drink

Real food can sometimes be used, but it is not always practicable. Sometimes players have to talk through their eating; moist foods, easily swallowed, are advisable. Coloured jellies, thick corn-flour, and custard can be disguised to represent many dishes. Sliced fruit can similarly form the basis of meat, poultry, etc., but large joints and hams are best made from papier mâché (see below). Bread-and-butter and sandwiches should be as thin as possible, and fillings, such as watercress, cucumber, or tomato, which are likely to put a player in difficulties, should be avoided. Hot water, poured over a stage "meal", can suggest hot food. A point is usually available back-stage for an electric kettle.

Tea, coffee, and cocoa can be real and freshly made, care being taken to ensure that the teapot holds sufficient to provide drink for all the players who have to take it. If tea cannot conveniently be made, a thermos flask can be used to keep a supply hot, the beverage being turned into the tea-pot or coffee-pot at the last moment. Beware of the skin on warmed milk. There is no convincing substitute for beer; therefore the real drink should be used. The use of real wines and spirits should be avoided: we *have* seen performances marred by the use of real intoxicants! Ginger ale looks like champagne. Water or lemonade can be tinted with cochineal or burnt sugar to look like wine. A small amount of bottled coffee will turn water into whisky or brandy, and diluted plum-juice can be a pleasant substitute for port wine. For gin, plain water is sufficient.

Telephones

These can often be borrowed from the telephone company free of charge, provided mention is made of the courtesy in the programme. Telephone connection should follow the lines of an actual installation. If the phone is away from a wall, the wire should run down to the floor, where, if it is visible to the audience, it should finish at a terminal block, i.e. a small piece of painted wood. If real electrical connection is made with an effects panel (see Chapter V), the phone should be sited as near the flat as possible to avoid a length of wire trailing across the floor: a mat can sometimes be used to cover the wire and to keep it out of the way of awkward feet.

Papier Mâché

This useful material can be used to make numerous properties, from a grape to a tree-trunk. Therefore its preparation and use are described in detail.

There are two main methods: (1) the shape is made by successive layers of paste-soaked strips of paper laid one on the other, partly overlapping, and the whole being allowed to dry; (2) shredded paper is pulped with paste, modelled, and allowed to dry. The first method is suitable for properties such as joints of meat, headgear, animal heads, logs, tree-trunks, images, large vases and jars. The basic shape is made with crumpled newspaper, disciplined, if necessary, with string or wire. Objects such as tree trunks require a stronger framework of chicken-wire, reinforced, if necessary, with wooden struts. Over this base are placed soaked strips torn (not cut) 2–3 ins. wide. (Heavily glazed paper is unsuitable.) Cold water paste of a creamy consistency is suitable. The strips should overlap, and, occasionally, the surface of the model should be brushed over with a brush loaded with paste. For extra strength, a few glued strips of rag can be used with the paper. The final thickness varies with the size of the model, and ranges from ⅛ in. to ½ in. While it is still wet, the shape can be modelled to a small extent with the fingers by pinching out or building up. Papier mâché made by the second method (see below) can be added and modelled. When the object is dry, it can be sandpapered and painted. This method can be used for reproducing shapes from moulds, such as bowls, plaques, or clay models. The articles should be oiled and a layer of unpasted paper applied. The paper should be torn into small pieces, pasted, and smoothed on to the

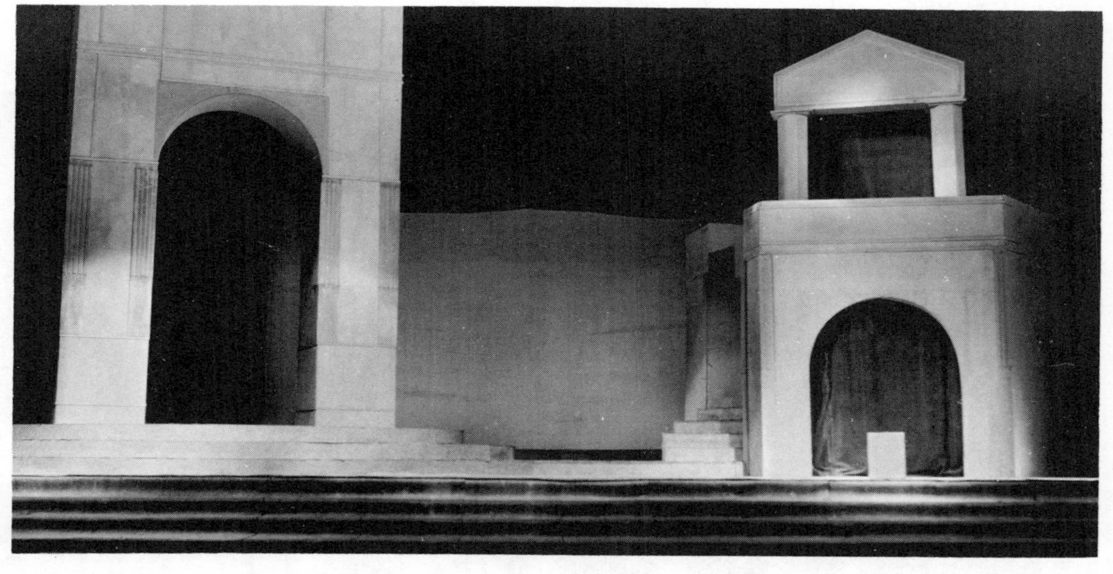

A simple but adequate set, typical of many college productions. This one was used for the Hofstra College's production of "Julius Caesar."

Courtesy ANTA

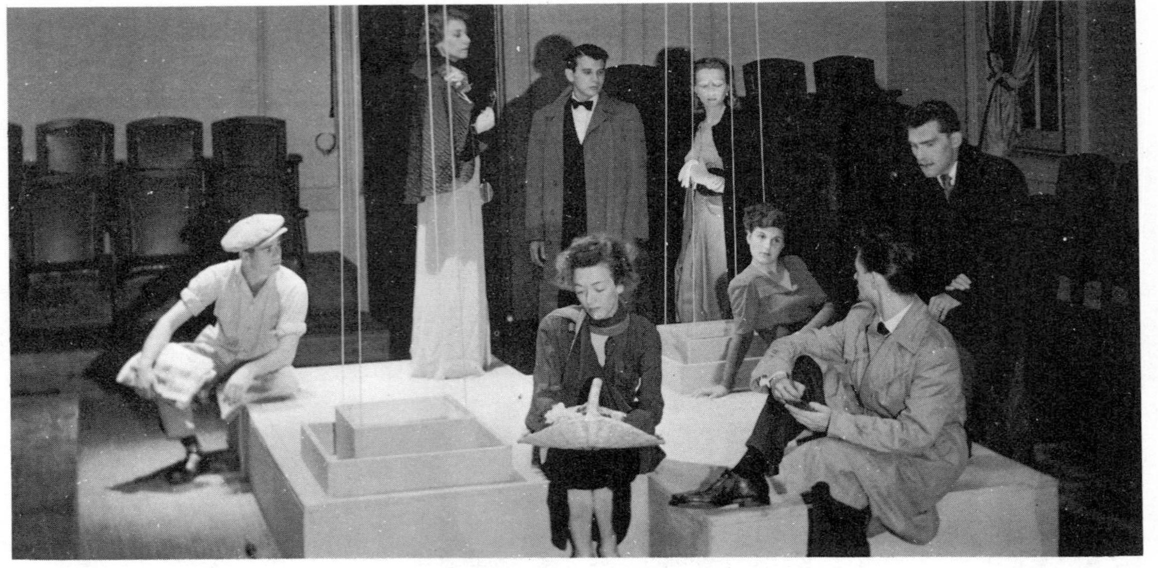

A rehearsal for Shaw's "Pygmalion," at the Gallery Circle Theatre, New Orleans, La. Note the seats surrounding the "stage."

Courtesy ANTA

article, care being taken to press well into any decorative feature. This should continue until about $\frac{1}{8}$ in. thickness is obtained. If the mâché is applied to the inside of a mould, it can be left to dry before being removed, but if it "surrounds" the model, it should be removed while still wet, filled with crumpled newspaper, and rejoined with more overlapping paste-strips.

For small objects, or for making decorative reliefs or detailed small shapes, the second method is preferable. The paper is torn into shreds and soaked for 24 hours; boiling helps to pulp the mixture. The surplus water is squeezed out, and to two cupsful of this mixture one of paste powder is added, the whole being kneaded and pummelled until the pulp adheres. There should be sufficient moisture in the pulp to mix the paste; if not, water should be added sparingly. Kneading can be done with a short length of broomstick and a bowl. The mixture is ready if a smooth surface, free from lumps, is obtained when the back of a spoon is drawn across it, and if it retains its shape when modelled. Powdered whiting or ordinary household flour must be added and thoroughly mixed; otherwise the preparation will be too sticky to handle. When modelling, the hands can be rubbed in flour to keep them from sticking. When modelled, the article should be allowed to dry slowly, although to hasten the process it can be placed in an oven at low temperature. There will be a slight shrinkage in drying. Small cavities that appear on drying can be filled with "Alabastine." When thoroughly dry, the object can be sandpapered, sized, and painted.

Experiment with papier mâché is essential. First efforts will not always be successful, but once the technique is mastered it is extremely useful and inexpensive.

With all properties the golden rule is that they shall appear to be right under stage conditions. What is right in real life may not be correct on the stage as is evidenced by the appearance of the natural complexion when it is seen under strong lighting. Experiment is the best guide. There is the story of the critic who adversely criticized a weapon as being unconvincing and out of period. Later the S.M. no doubt with some triumph, showed him the gun. It bore the year and place of manufacture, both of which were in strict accordance with the play: but the critic may still have been right.

CHAPTER V

EFFECTS

EFFECTS consist of any unusual sounds or special visual features that occur on or off the stage during a performance. The methods that are adopted to achieve effects are many. We offer ideas and a few hints, and warn against the use of effects for "effects' sake." Undue novelty can distract an audience, and theatrical devices that are not essentials can well be omitted. For example, it may be wiser to dispense with thunder and lightning if the noise *sounds* like a thunder sheet and the flash *looks* like the flicking of a switch. Unconvincing effects mark amateur status.

Sound effects can either be obtained on records, or be manual, i.e. produced by means of hand-operated appliances. Whichever method is used, the sound should appear to come from its appropriate source, and should not drown dialogue. These obvious precautions are often overlooked. Conversely, scenery, curtains, and people deaden sound and allowances must be made for this fact. Only experiment can give the S.M. his correct effect, and if it is not possible to rehearse under the conditions of the final performance, it is better to under-do rather than over-do the effect.

Recorded effects are increasingly popular with amateurs. A turntable and amplifier (sometimes known as a panatrope) with two speakers form the equipment. This can be hired, bought, or, perhaps, made if a skilled radio engineer is available. The equipment should be as portable as possible. Of the two speakers, one is usually used in front of the curtains for incidental music, and the other back-stage for effects. The plugs of these two speakers should be of different colours so that the S.M. can easily identify the leads, and make certain that the correct speaker is in use.

Using the Amplifier

Most sound effects are obtainable on records; the sound effects for the whole of some popular plays are available on one record. Each effect is separated on the record by a narrow, smooth band, and it is advisable to number, or mark, this this in white Indian ink in order to identify the different sections. All records should be clearly marked with a stick-on label that gives the title and any special features that should be noted. Placing the needle in the correct groove calls for practice. It should be rehearsed at an early stage, and not left to be "tacked on" either at the dress rehearsal or public performance. Under-rehearsal will shake the confidence not only of the S.M., but also of members of the cast, who are easily put off by unaccustomed noises. The volume should be turned down before the needle is placed in the groove, and then increased as necessary. This is ascertained by experiment, and when it is decided, the dial reading should be noted. It can also be marked with chalk, or by cribbage pegs inserted in drilled holes in the dial. Volume can vary with the type of needle used. Some records are satisfactory only when used with a light-weight pick-up.

It is useful to have a simple rack to hold the records during a performance; when left about, they are easily broken, and amplifying apparatus gives off heat that damages them. Often, however, the deep lid fitted to most amplifiers suffices. It is advisable to watch the wear and tear of a record as an over-worked disc may produce little else than a scratchy noise. A further warning is: recordings, even of the same music or effect, sometimes vary. We rehearsed for weeks with a record and obtained a new one for the performance but during the check-up on the night the new record itself, "swung," dragged badly, and had to be abandoned. Nothing should be left to chance.

Record labels usually remind users that re-playing to the public is copyright and that permission should first be obtained.

A microphone can be used with an amplifier. It is not essential but it can be useful for special effects such as the "telephone" or "radio" voice, crackling fire (using crumpled "Cellophane" paper) and many more interesting sounds that are discovered by experiment. But a microphone is apt to be temperamental, and a thorough try-out beforehand is essential. Care must be taken that the actual voice is not heard from the wings—only the reproduced sound—and when several people are speaking into the microphone, it must be ascertained how near and at what angle they need to be to the instrument; they may also have to alter their voices to suit its range.

We have seen microphones hopefully "concealed" about the stage to amplify the voices of the cast. Uniformity of volume can seldom be obtained by this method, and often a double-voice is heard by members of the audience who are close to the speakers; in any event, no dramatic society worthy of its name should resort to these measures.

Manual Effects

These are numerous. We describe a few of the commoner types. An S.M. will develop a keen ear for sounds of everyday life that can be reproduced simply for any future plays and he can be well occupied, between productions, in experimenting.

Bells

For the modern door-bell the actual bell can be rigged up by an amateur or, more simply, the small units (battery, bell, and push) can be bought, but care must be taken to operate the bell where the ring is supposed to be heard; the siting of a bell may call for "remote control," in which case the battery and switch are mounted on a board placed in a convenient position —if necessary, hung round the S.M.'s neck. Such a bell is useful for recalling an audience between acts. Striking clock —or heavy—bells can be represented by a length of solid-drawn piping, the tone of which can be altered by shortening or drilling. It is suspended perpendicularly by one length of rope and struck with a piece of padded wood. Another length of rope is attached to the lower end and held. (If suspended from one end, and not steadied, a pendulum momentum is liable to be set up as the pipe is struck repeatedly; this can be difficult to control.) Undue reverberation can be checked by grasping the piping. The old-fashioned school handbell can be useful, and, if it is correctly swung, can give the effect of the spring-mounted bell that was used in Victorian houses. The modern tubular chiming bells can be transferred complete to the wings and struck by hand to give this rather distinctive effect.

Door Knocker

Too often this consists of banging a heavy object on the floor of the stage. A real knocker should be mounted on a board and tried out against a wall, a door, or the floor.

Slamming Door

A real door should be slammed, if possible. Alternatively, a length of wood 4 ft. by 6 ins. is used. Rope is attached to one end with a screw-eye and held by the operator; the board is laid on the floor flat, one foot is placed on it, the other behind; it is then lifted and released to strike the floor. (See Figure 22.) A piece of sprung steel at the bottom of the board will give the double click effect usually heard when a door closes. If the sound is too "hard," a piece of carpet should be used to muffle the blow.

Horses

Coco-nut shells cannot be bettered, but they require practice. If neighing is also required, a record is safer, unless a talented impersonator is available.

Gravel Paths

A large wooden tray is filled with gravel and walked on, the operator "marking time"; or heavy wire mesh ("chain link" fencing) is placed between two thick cardboard sheets and walked on.

Broken Glass

This should be real broken glass (obtainable from a builder's nerchant); it can be poured from one box into another. It ieeds careful handling. Large-scale crash effects are best obtained by recordings.

Crowds and Voices Off-stage

Small crowds can usually be represented by the members of he cast and stage-staff, but they should be rehearsed in the use f actual words and speeches. Vague, impromptu mumblings re not convincing.

Thunder and Lightning

A sheet of thin metal-plate (sometimes used to back the ousehold sink) is suspended by means of a piece of thick ring and shaken for a crackle effect. (See Figure 23.) Tin-late is not satisfactory. A drum roll, or an open cistern tank umbled with a padded hammer, is necessary for the echo. he effect of sheet (reflected) lightning can be achieved by icking light switches. If this involves the noisy clicking of nap switches (lightning precedes thunder), it may be possible make and break electrical contact by means of a connecting lug, which can be set so that slight pushing and withdrawing an give the flicker without noise. If the switchboard is fitted ith sliding dimmer controls, these can be moved up and down ith an irregular motion. Other, more complicated, methods f getting a lightning effect are possible, but these are best left an electrician.

istol Shot and Gun Fire

Bamboo cane brought down on a leather, or similar, chair ill suffice, or a starting pistol can be used. For heavy, distant unfire the tank or drum is required (an inverted plywood tea-hest will sometimes do service as a drum). For machine-un fire, a bird-scaring rattle (as used by football fans) should tried out, the rattle being turned slowly by hand and not vung.

Fig. 22: Door Slam and method of using.

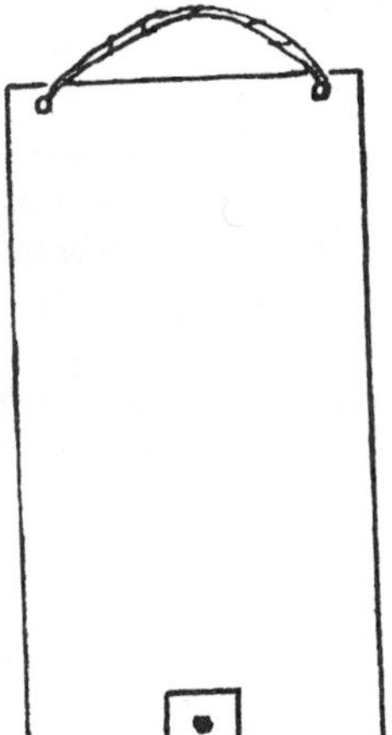

Fig. 23: Thunder Sheet.

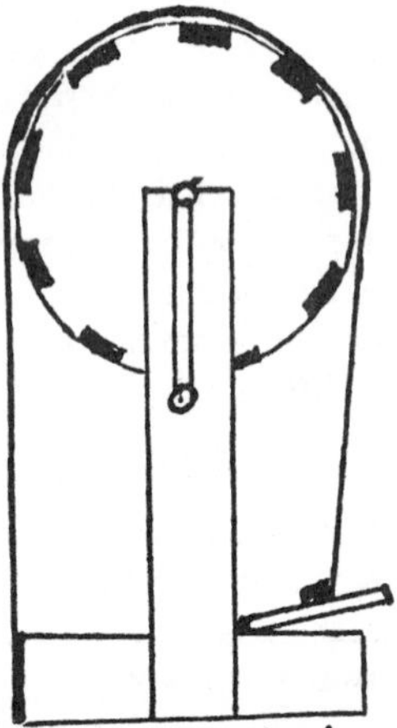

Fig. 24: Wind Machine (end vie

Fireworks

The hissing sound of a rocket or squib-type firework is best done by voices in the wings (hissing through clenched teeth). This is followed by the report, which can often be convincingly suggested by the bursting of a paper bag. Or the pistol can be used. The coloured glow effect of some fireworks can be obtained by a coloured floodlight controlled by a dimmer switch, or by striking coloured matches.

Surf and Waves

A large round tray (a converted sieve will do) is loaded with small lead shot, which is swished around by a circular movement. For effects of only a short period, however, a recording which can include the cry of gulls will give more atmosphere.

Rice grains will similarly give the sound of spray, and, if dropped into the tray suddenly from a low position, can give the impression of a body or object falling into water.

Rain

A handful of dried peas or lead shot can be rotated on a drum or in a fine-mesh sieve. An ordinary tray or a cardboard lid (gown boxes are often available in the dressing-room) can sometimes be used to obtain a similar effect, but, because of the oblong shape, the steady sound required is less easily controlled. To obtain the visual effect of rain, rice is allowed to fall steadily, preferably lighted by a spot light. If the visible area is large, a long trough, with holes through which the rice is allowed to fall, is required. In practice, this is apt to be complicated. If rain *must* be seen, we suggest that the S.M. should have his window space small, and covered, if the play permits, with net curtain.

Wind

This is created by a wind machine, which consists of a wooden drum on a stand. The drum is slatted, and stretched over it is a piece of canvas, weighted at one end and anchored to the framework at the other. The drum is revolved by means of a handle. If the free end is pulled down, the sound is heavier. This can be done by hand or by connecting the end with ropes and a treadle which can be controlled with the foot. (See Figure 24.) The faster the drum revolves, the higher the "wind." The visual effect of wind (usually moving curtains) can be obtained by wafting air with a large sheet of ply or boarding. For steady effects an electric fan is needed.

Fog

A series of fine mesh nettings, known as gauze or scrim, lowered from the "grid" at intervals, can give the effect of thickening fog, but this may not be possible with a small society. Actual fog can be made by pouring hot water over "Cardice" or "Dri-Kold" (frozen air) obtainable in block form from ice-cream merchants. This must not be touched with the bare hand or blisters will result. The vapour produced can be wafted on to the stage. The S.M. must remember that such fog will probably need dispersing, before the next scene, by smothering the block with old sacking and removing it, and by ventilating the stage thoroughly. Failing these methods it is best to rely on subdued lighting and the acting skill of the cast.

Snow

For large, continuous effects, a snow trough is needed. This is made of canvas with holes through which the snow (torn white paper) is allowed to fall (the paper can be varnished to make it glisten). As with rain, given a small, slightly obscured window, the "snow" can be dropped by hand. Should a door be open to reveal the outside, then the snow must appear there too!

Trains

Sandpaper blocks rubbed together, or blowing direct into a microphone, will take a "train" out of the station, but recorded effects of all train noises are so much more realistic that they should be used.

Cars

Car noises are best recorded, but the modern car is certainly not noisy and the effect can often be omitted without loss of realism. A door slam can often suggest a car drawn up or about to pull away. The screech of brakes can be produced by the squeak of air forced through compressed lips, using a microphone with adequate rehearsal!

Water

Old clothes and properties of no value, if treated with varnish and allowed to dry, will appear wet. An umbrella can be treated in this way.

Lighting

We merely touch on this important branch of stagecraft as the subject is adequately covered by a separate handbook in this Series.

The lighting equipment of a small hall is usually limited to two or three "battens" of overhead lights and a row of footlights. The lamps used are not usually coloured and the S.M. may need to supply coloured gelatines, the detailed uses and effects of which cannot be dealt with here. Auxiliary lighting is obtained by floodlights, which can flood the stage with light or be used to illuminate back-cloths, and spot lights, which pick out a very small area. This is the basic equipment with which the S.M. must usually achieve his effects. The lights are controlled by ordinary tumbler switches, or sometimes by sliding resistance switches that enable the lights to vary from zero to full brightness. These are known as dimmers. Gradual sunsets, sunrises, darkening skies, etc., call for their use.

The counsel of adequate preparation and rehearsal applies even more strongly to lighting, for the pitfalls are many. For example, a total black-out is often impossible owing to exit lights near the stage. Switches can be noisy and destroy illusion; a thick duster may help to muffle them. Often only part of the equipment is connected to dimmers, imported equipment which runs from sockets or dips, is not. The operation of the switchboard itself often requires a small working light owing to darkness in the wings, but this light must not "leak" on to the stage in dark scenes. Flexes can trip the unwary, lamps can fail, and fuses can blow. House (audience) lights are sometimes controlled by switches both in the hall and back-stage. Stage lighting may suit everybody except the prompter who may sometimes find his corner in semi-darkness. We do not intend to discourage experiment, or to suggest that lighting is bound to prove a nuisance, but there are factors that the efficient S.M. should bear in mind. Small precautions, such as putting a switch out of action with adhesive tape, chalking clearly on the switchboard what lights are controlled, etc., covering loose flex with a mat, having a torch handy, and so on, may prevent an effect being spoiled.

Fires, Lamps, and Candles

These are really properties, but we introduce them here because they rely on effects. A fire should be built up realistically, using logs, coal, and gelatines (coloured transparent sheets) of the right colour, supported by wire netting and lit by one or more light bulbs. A flicker effect can be obtained by centring a small propeller-shaped piece of metal on a pivot over the lamp (as found in some modern electric fires); the heat of the bulbs causes this to revolve, giving the effect of a moving light.

The same effect can be achieved by a fluorescent light starter-fuse run in circuit. The lower the wattage of the bulb, the greater the flicker. This is often more convenient than the propeller method, which calls for precision adjustment. If the S.M. is not familiar with the term "run in circuit," an electrician should be consulted.

Real flame is not allowed on the stage, and portable oil lamps, storm lamps, etc., should be converted into battery-operated lights. The S.M. could experiment with the small dimmer switches obtainable from war department surplus stores; these switches can be fitted to replace the normal wick control. Electric candles can be bought or hired, but an ordinary cylindrical pencil torch built up with crepe paper will often suffice. The candle-stick may be so constructed as to allow the "candle" to be pushed down into it, thus creating the illusion of its burning away. The introduction of such portable lights calls for appropriate lighting changes, but detailed treatment of this subject is outside the scope of this book.

CHAPTER VI

REHEARSALS

THE professional S.M. is not expected to be present a rehearsals, but the amateur S.M. is, as he can then get t know the play thoroughly and keep a check on the produce players, and prompter. During the last few rehearsals th S.M. should be in a position to take over from the produce if necessary—hence the importance of his script. He shoul see that the cast can handle properties, or substitutes, and tha they mime opening and closing doors, etc., as soon as word are learnt and the rehearsals are well under way. Before eac rehearsal the outline of the set and positions of the mai furniture should be marked with chalk (actual furniture can b used if available), or some means should be found to get th cast used to performance conditions. The producer may b glad of help in keeping the cast "up to scratch," i.e. arrivin on time, maintaining silence during rehearsal, and being read to enter on their cues. A special word about the prompter desirable. Prompting is often handed over to a newcomer c to the odd-man-out, especially if the group is small. Prompting is an important job, and the prompter can be encourage to develop a sense of responsibility not limited to an occasion correction or prompt "on the night." During rehearsals th actors' moves should be noted by the prompter, using th right-hand column of the prompt copy, in pencil; pauses mu be marked in the actual text by means of a symbol; (e.g. agreed on by the producer, S.M., and prompter. The prompt should get used to observing when an actor is in difficulty wit his words; to do this he will have to watch the scene as we as follow the text: the symptom of distress may be a blan look or a glance thrown towards the defaulter by anoth player. Unfortunately, in rehearsals the cast gets into the habit of calling on the prompter verbally, usually with an apology. This is unfair to the prompter. Trick warnings such as coughs, movements of the hands, etc., should be avoided: they are the mark of bad workmanship and are usually detected. When the prompter has to give a cue, he should give it clearly and in the intonation of the speech. Some players prefer a key word or phrase to be given to them, but the actual words forgotten are safer. In the event of a muddled speech, the experienced prompter will skip the tangled section and give a cue further on that suggests a new train of thought; it may even be necessary to cut out the speech altogether and to give a cue to another speaker. Small inaccuracies should be pointed out to the players after a scene; the action should not be interrupted. During final rehearsals the producer may also wish to dispense with the prompter and to make his cast improvise their way through difficulties. Finally, all members of the group should at some time have experience at prompting.

Effects should be used as early as possible, not only for the sake of practice but also so that the cast can get used to having them as a background, speaking "over" them, if necessary. Also some effects, such as pistol shots, can be startling especially if they are omitted until the actual performance. As the cast becomes word-perfect, the actual cue-word for placing the needle in the groove, ringing the bell, etc., can be marked; previous warning cues will also be needed, and if the S.M. will be working with helpers, he must rehearse his system of communication, be it whispered instruction, hand signal, or numbered reference card held up in view of the operator of the lights or effect. Some theatres have a system of "cue-lights," one colour for the warning and one for the actual operation, wired from the prompt corner to the operator, but unless thoroughly rehearsed these are best left alone. At final rehearsals the S.M. should try to position his helpers as they will be on the night.

Before the dress rehearsal the play should have been timed

—each act and scene with its intervals, the incidental music, estimated scene-changing, etc. The timing of a costume-change within a scene must not be overlooked, nor must the distance from stage to dressing-room be forgotten; and if the voice of the player who is changing is to be heard off-stage, it may be necessary for a "stand-in" to speak for him.

It is a good idea to have a S.M.'s rehearsal a few days before the dress rehearsal proper. At this the cast can rehearse their costume-changing and the S.M. his scene-changing, effects, property drill, etc. This differs from the dress rehearsal in that interpretation and artistic considerations are secondary; probably stretches of dialogue can be cut. Nevertheless, on the stage management side absolute discipline and routine are essential. At this stage the producer should be unnecessary, but any orders from him to the S.M.'s helpers should be given through the S.M. The cast should not interfere with properties that are not their concern; they should be out of the way but within call. Some effects, etc., will not be possible, failing the use of the hall for this rehearsal, but lighting changes can be called out—perhaps mimed—and a portable gramophone can give correct timing for recordings.

As the full dress-rehearsal should follow the lines of the actual performance to the public (discussed in the next chapter) it need not be dealt with separately, but one or two points may be given. Dress rehearsals are usually long and trying, and the members should be warned accordingly. A bad dress-rehearsal does not mean a good performance; probably some dress rehearsals have been so bad that any subsequent performance has seemed wonderful in comparison—hence the superstition! Nevertheless, the group should not be too discouraged by events. The company may think this an appropriate time for stage photographs, and if this is the province of the S.M., he should have his "pictures" clearly in mind. Much valuable time can be wasted by impromptu groupings with an overwrought cast.

As this is probably the final meeting of the company before "the night," extra care must be taken to see that all hand properties are in order and in the right hands, available for collection, if necessary (though it is usually best for the cast to be responsible for their own at this stage). Stage properties should be carefully checked and stacked, or packed, and ready for transport to the theatre—or they should be stored in the wings if the dress rehearsal has been held there. Finally, the cast and back-stage helpers should receive clear instructions on their responsibilities and the general procedure "on the night."

CHAPTER VII

ON THE NIGHT

THE more preliminaries that can be got over *before* the night of the public performance, the better. (Here we assume a routine that may actually begin some days before "the night.")

Scenery and properties should be loaded methodically and checked. Small properties should be contained in large boxes, cases, etc., especially if they are fragile. Glassware will require protective packing (newspapers screwed up). Expensive equipment should be left to the last, or conveyed separately in a car. All this may be a contractor's responsibility, but the S.M. should supervise, or delegate supervision. Scenery is sometimes struck and loaded late at night after a show, in which case a working light on the lorry will be useful.

Meanwhile, the stage should have been cleared and swept and the S.M. should then draw a rough plan of the set with chalk on the floor, deciding on a point for erecting his first flat (e.g. a door or window may have to be in a particular spot), though if his preliminary survey work and plans are correct the siting should be accurate automatically.

Erecting a Set

The first flat should be placed in position and braced on both sides to hold it rigid; the next flat is then placed edge to edge with the first, following the chalkline. The two are then lashed, i.e. tied together, using the rope and cleats. (See Figure 12, Chapter III.) Throwing the line over the top cleat needs practice, but if the knack is mastered, the time-wasting use of steps is avoided. This procedure is followed with each flat until the set is erected, after which, strategic points (e.g. behind doors, corners, etc.) should be braced. Should the screwing down of the braces into the floor be difficult (e.g. shallow parquet flooring is liable to split and some stage-boarding is too thin to screw into), sandbags or brace-weights should be used to hold them down.

Brace-weights can be made from scrap lead-piping, or cable, melted down. These, and the braces, are best painted white to make them show up in the dim light back-stage. When all flats are in position, any gaps at the joins should be sealed; this is called "stripping the join," and it is usually done by gluing or pinning strips of linen or old sacking behind the joins, but this is not advised if there are scene changes during the play. With the fibre-boarding flats these gaps are less likely. If gaps at the top of the flats are due to the rake of the stage, the back flats will have to lean forward slightly to fit those at the sides. Where flats are set at an angle to the rake gaps will appear at the bottom; one of these flats will then require to be packed at its base to tilt it into a correct position.

The clearance of the doors and french windows should be checked and practical windows should be tested. With an assistant moving in the auditorium checking on lines of sight, the backings should be placed into position. Make sure the cast have room to move in and out of the doors without squeezing. Any rostra or stairs should then be positioned; if a rostrum leads off-stage, it should not stop abruptly just out of sight of the audience or the cast will glance down as they use it; a table, a few desks, or even a chair, will help the player to walk off safely and convincingly. Stairs and rostra should be tested for stability and strength, especially if a player has to run up or down. Excessive ladder work is tiring and a ladder or steps should be used methodically, special precautions being taken with a raked stage. It will be needed to hang curtains, pelmets, and the borders, if these are necessary. One or more borders may be required to hide the "grid" from the audience, and should be tested from the centre of the front row; these are usually in the form of curtains, 2 ft. wide, stretched across the width of the stage.

The stage should now be ready for "dressing"; the carpet, if any, is laid, the pictures hung, and the furniture put into position, in consultation with the producer. *Stage* properties, such as clocks, vases, ash trays, etc., can be set out, but *hand* properties used by the cast are best kept away from the stage; they should be accessible and easily checked.

Lighting should then be tested. A model should walk about the stage, and the S.M. should observe the effect. If the stage has an "apron," it may be necessary to warn the cast not to use it, as, unless there are corrective front-of-house lights, they are likely to move into shadow. Floodlights should be adjusted, and if any are used to light back-cloths and are behind the set, all other lights should be dimmed and the S.M. should stand in the auditorium and test for gaps and general effect. Floodlights have vents that sometimes give a light-leakage; they can be shielded but not blocked, for their purpose is to ventilate and cool the light. Cables to floods and spots should be slung across the grid, if possible, and not trailed across the floor. All light switches should be tested, and the lighting cues gone over with the assistant, who must have his cue-sheet to hand; if time allows, a run-through of the cues with lighting changes should be taken. Lights, particularly floods and spots, should not be left on unnecessarily for the lamps have a limited life.

Attention must now be given to the amplifier, making sure that it is not linked with the lighting circuits (or if it is, that precautions are taken to keep its control separate). An amplifier and turntable should be given time to warm up. Each speaker should be tested separately. If only one is available to cope with effects from various points, it should be placed centrally at the back of the stage. Half-way down the hall the S.M. should listen and give instructions about the volume, remembering to allow for the talking and shuffling of the audience during intervals, and for the damping effect of a crowded house. Music, or effects, with dialogue should then be tried out; the rule is that the speech takes precedence. If the dialogue can be heard over the recorded sound at about three-quarters of the way down the hall, it is likely to be satisfactory.

The cast should now be invited to come on the stage to "get the feel of it" and to try out their voices, etc. They should not be allowed to move furniture or properties unless instructed to do so by the producer and S.M., and they should be warned of any danger spots (tricky doors, obstacles, unlighted areas, etc., which may be unavoidable, even in the best-organized production). The cast should then be sent off to get ready (most of them should already be made up, as the producer should be able to test make-up under stage lights), and stage properties not already on the stage should be carefully arranged in the wings—preferably on a table. If possible, they should be marked with the act, scene, and character who will use them. There should also be a final check with the cast responsible for their own hand properties.

If the hall-doors are not secured, a watch must be kept on early arrivals, for members of the audience should not see the stage with curtains open. When the curtains are drawn, they should be tested thoroughly, then left alone. Peeping through them "isn't done".

Front-of-house stewards should be at the ready and know their cue for "house lights off" and the cast should be given periodical warnings of time, the last being about five minutes before curtain time, when the foot-lights should be put on to "settle" the audience. The final instruction will be "on stage!" The S.M. may want the cast to remain in the dressing-room until their call. This may certainly ease pressure on wing-space. However, most amateurs prefer to watch their colleagues and they are more likely to catch the atmosphere of the play if they witness its progress, but they should remain in absolute silence in the wings. See also that the prompter is comfortably settled and ready. He should have a torch handy. The cast and stage-helpers are then told to "stand-by." If any member is not ready, there should be a clear reply "not ready," and no panic.

A prompt start creates a good impression; late beginnings

are all too common amongst amateurs. As the public judge the time from the hall clock, the S.M.'s own watch and timing should synchronize with it. Late-comers should not be pandered to; the society has a duty to its loyal—and prompt—fans as well as to the privileged, but sometimes late, front-row-V.I.P.s.

For a good start we suggest the following drill: HIT lights for Act I, Scene I, FADE incidental music, KILL house-lights, FADE in curtain music, CURTAIN, fade music (to "hit" and "kill" lights is to put them on or off); if the play does not have to open immediately with dialogue, the audience should be given a few seconds to absorb the scene; it may be, and should be, their only opportunity of appreciating the S.M.'s labours.

During the play, back-stage work should proceed calmly but cheerfully; this may help to reassure a nervous cast. If players are to need assistants for quick costume changes, these should be at the alert. Members of the cast should be particularly warned about moving to their dressing-rooms quietly at the end of their own appearance, or of the scene. Release of tension often produces high-pitched and audible voices. Intervals should be covered by suitable music, during which scene changes are effected, using the plan, if necessary. The cast should not be on the stage. Two minutes before the end of the intervals the audience should be recalled by a bell and the opening routine repeated. Intervals between acts call for house lights to be put on, but for breaks between scenes, the auditorium should be left in darkness.

After the final curtain, curtain calls are usually taken. These should be rehearsed and the atmosphere of the play held, if possible. Wigs should not be removed, and curtain calls should not be repeated unless applause warrants repetition. After the National Anthem the audience should hear suitably lively music; friends and relations should not be encouraged back-stage (either after or during the performance), nor should the cast appear at any time in costume or make-up outside the play. If further performances are to follow, a quick check is advisable before the members of the cast go home. Ideally, everything should be set ready for the following night's performance.

This is not a rigid routine; local conditions and the number of helpers vary, but some routine, preparation, and "benevolent dictatorship" are essential to a smooth production. We have not dwelt on either the humorous or the human side of amateur productions. The keen S.M. will think of many things that we have not mentioned—the first-aid box, the beaker and carafe of drinking water in the wings for dry or nervous throats, the word of encouragement, the packet of throat pastilles, the handy pocket mirror, the packet of safety pins, and a confident smile despite everything. A happy team is often a good team, and successful amateur dramatic work is essentially a corporate effort.

CHAPTER VIII

THE DRAMA FESTIVAL

The Festival

A DRAMA festival consists of the performance of one-act plays and lasts from one or two days to a week. After the performances each evening an adjudicator comments on the performances and generally gives advice to the entrants. The adjudication is public. The S.M.'s society may enter such a festival and he may find himself appointed a festival S.M. Therefore, we deal with these two specialized aspects of stagecraft.

Festivals may be competitive or non-competitive. In competitive festivals marks, based on the standard of the production, acting, etc., are given. The section that chiefly concerns the S.M. is usually known as "Stage Presentation," for which a maximum of 10 per cent of the marks is allotted. Stage Presentation includes the design and effectiveness of the set, the lighting, costumes, make-up, and effects. Although 10 per cent may seem a small proportion of the total, it should be remembered that an efficient, perhaps inspired, setting, may stimulate the cast, improve the production, and generally contribute to dramatic achievement. Also poorly timed effects and mismanaged properties may adversely affect the performance, so the S.M. should not estimate his share in the festival performance at a mere tenth.

Planning

The general principles of stage management set out in previous chapters apply to festivals, but there may be important differences. The script will be prepared in the usual way. The stage survey may have to be carried out in a modified form and in conjunction with the festival organizers; usually they supply the competing society with full particulars of lighting, properties, plan of the stage, etc. There will also be regulations that apply to time limits for setting, playing, and striking the play, the number of back-stage helpers, the type of additional scenery allowed, etc. These should be carefully borne in mind when the play is chosen and during the rehearsals.

The Festival Set

Most festival authorities stipulate a basic curtain set, which they provide, and allow one or more flats to suggest the scene. There are not usually any restrictions about furniture; it is safer for a team to supply its own and to be sure of its suitability, but the organizers often provide a few basic pieces, together with one or more rostra. If using the festival's furniture, the S.M. should see it in good time and assure himself that it is suitable for his play.

An adjudicator will not expect a high degree of realism under festival conditions, but he will look for the effective suggestion, artistic arrangement, and, if the type of play permits, colour and originality. These must be achieved with a scene that is capable of being quickly set and struck. The curtains themselves can be effectively arranged. They can be bunched together, for example, to produce a pillar effect, being fastened to the floor with drawing pins or being placed in boxes that represent plinths. Such adaptation will need backing, as will entrances and exits (unless the curtains are arranged to obviate this. (See Chapter III.) A door, fireplace, or window flat can be inserted in the curtain set simply by drawing the curtains aside and placing the flat in position.

It may be necessary to bring a curtain to the level of the top of the flat, in which case it can be shortened by rolling, the roll being away from the audience. There should be no attempt to make the curtains look like walls, etc., and pictures should not be hung on them. If possible, the flats should harmonize with the curtain surround, either matching or contrasting. It is wise not to overdo the use of flats, as the result may be inartistic. They need not be used only as inserts; a flat on its side can represent a brick wall, or a groundrow (see Figure 27), or an upright flat can jut out from the side curtains to represent the end of a house. The keen S.M. will soon discover numerous ways of getting the best out of the limited provision at festivals.

It follows that the society should look for a play that gives scope for simple, but effective, staging, bearing in mind that it is the one-act play festival that provides opportunities in the amateur theatre for experimental work in stagecraft as well as authorship and production. As there is little financial return, the stage management should not be expensive. For an example of such plays we illustrate the sets of three festival one-act plays that have been performed by the authors' own dramatic group. (See Figures 25, 26, and 27.) In the preliminary performances of the first play the pillars were represented by curtains (see above) and a blue back-cloth was used.

When the play was performed at probably one of the largest town-hall stages in the country this would not work, for all drapes and fittings were in unrelieved black. The theme and setting of the play was Greek, and, therefore, simplicity and dignity were keynotes—hence the simple design shown was possible. Pillars were made from cereal cartons, flattened out, the seat from packing cases, plywood, and hessian. The rostra were covered with ceiling paper; the cost of the whole came to well under a pound. The height of the stage necessitated the pillars being made on the "extended flat" method (see Chapter III), and were thus usable for a number of subsequent performances at smaller halls. Figure 26 shows a simple setting using one door flat mounted on a rostrum and fronted with a small unit of stairs; the properties shown in the sketch were dummy packets built into units with "Cellotape"; the bar was a cupboard with its back facing the audience, and behind it was another rostrum. Figure 27 shows a period set (Elizabethan) again. Three flats were used, two adjoining representing an inn, and one on

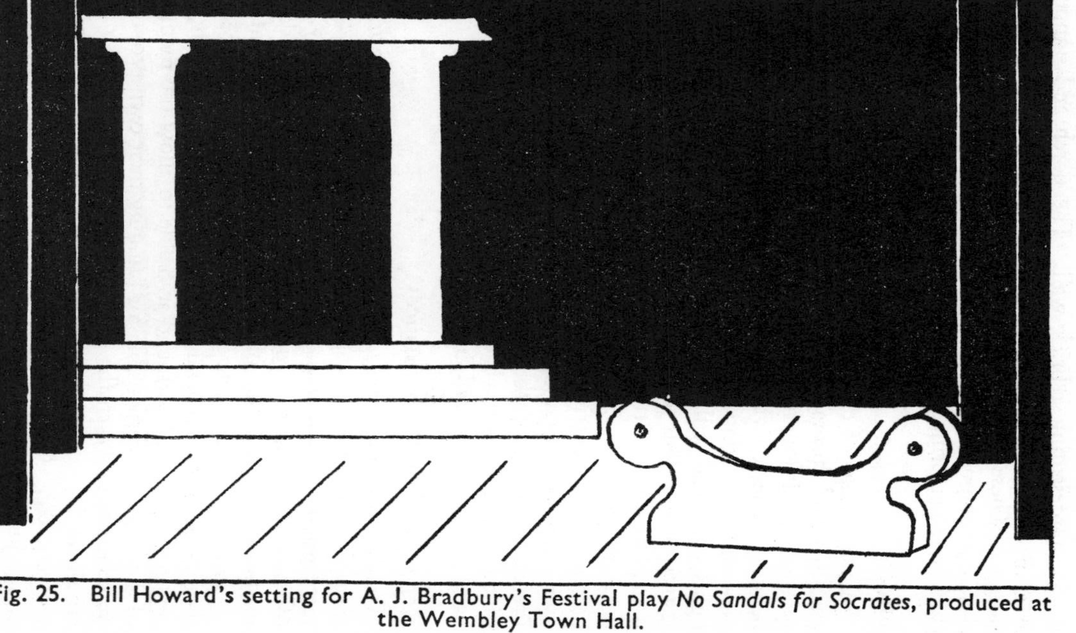

Fig. 25. Bill Howard's setting for A. J. Bradbury's Festival play *No Sandals for Socrates*, produced at the Wembley Town Hall.

its side representing a brick wall. The porch and signpost were made readily detachable by means of slotted socket fittings. These three settings were set and struck well within the limits imposed by the organizers of the festivals at which they were performed.

Effects

A wide range of effects is usually available at a festival: an amplifier and turntable, dimmer switchboard, and movable spotlights and floodlights form part of the equipment. (See below.) The festival organizers will require a copy of the play and a lighting plot. The actual manipulation of the lights and effects will sometimes be in the hands of the resident festival S.M. This plot will need careful preparation, for on it may depend the timing and correctness of the effects, and the S.M. can work efficiently only if he has clear information before him. Sometimes a marked text, following the S.M.'s own prepared script, can be supplied to the resident S.M. Preferably, however, the competing society should be responsible for as much of the back-stage work as possible. Second-hand, often unrehearsed, instructions, are risky.

Rehearsals and Performances

It is important to time accurately the length of the performance, for some festival authorities disqualify for an excess of mere minutes. Otherwise, rehearsals proceed normally, but often with increased intensity and more exacting standards, for herein lies the value of the festival. Firm but tactful discipline must be in evidence. On the night itself the procedure should follow the general lines set down in Chapter VII, excepting that it will be found advisable to allow the members of the cast to be responsible for bringing their own properties on to the stage when the scene is in position, and when they are allowed a quick try-out of doors, steps, windows, furniture drawers, etc. Only large properties should be kept in the wings just before the performance; small effects left lying about may be unwittingly removed by other teams.

Fig. 26. A. J. Bradbury's "Bar-room" setting to curtains for his Festival One-Act play *Air on the G String*.

Curtain cues are given by the festival S.M. and not the team's own S.M. Calm confidence before and during the play is vital. Prompts should be clear, and the cast should be warned to "act through" any technical hitches or dry-ups as naturally as possible. Forgotten lines in themselves are not likely to lose the team many points; it is the loss of illusion and dramatic effect that knocks off the marks.

At the end of the performance the team may have a duty towards other groups. The set should be struck without fuss and every facility given to the rival team that follows. Good sportsmanship should be a feature of competition in the amateur theatre no less than in the field of games and athletics.

The Festival Stage Manager

The stage management of an entire drama festival is a responsible, worth-while job that calls for tactful authority, organizing ability, and a keen interest in festival drama itself. More than any other member of the festival organizing committee does the S.M. come into contact with participating drama teams.

Thorough planning is essential. A wide choice of halls is not usual, but the festival S.M. should investigate the possibilities in his district, and be in a position to advise the committee should the question of choice arise. Front-of-house considerations are likely to take precedence, but the play and its effective presentation are equally important. A fairly large stage is desirable, and plenty of room in the wings will make for smooth running. Lighting can usually be augmented (but the capacity of the lighting system must not be overworked to the extent of fusing), and, if not already fitted, dimmer switch-boards can usually be inserted in the circuit. Storage space as near the stage as possible will be needed for the furniture and properties, which may have to serve many plays and not merely one evening's performance. If possible, the order of presenting the plays should be arranged to facilitate the movement of furniture, which should not be allowed to remain on the premises longer than necessary. Hence, in a

Fig. 27. Bill Howard's setting to curtains for T. B. Morris's One-Act play *The Tail of Fire* (Wembley Drama Guild Festival)

competitive festival with preliminaries and finals, where any team may be a finalist, the entire paraphernalia of all the teams is likely to accumulate by the evening when the finalists are decided upon; therefore, this type of festival should not be undertaken lightly.

The initial survey of the stage equipment and various facilities will have to be thorough. The committee will have to decide what furniture and equipment shall be made available to the teams. Typically this consists of the normal lighting equipment in the hall, plus portable floodlights and spotlights, some or all of the lights being connected with dimmers. Tables, chairs, rostra, and perhaps a divan, sideboard, or bureau usually suffice for the furniture. Well before the date of the festival the teams should be informed of the facilities and supplied with a plan of the stage in duplicate, one copy of which, showing details of the team's setting of the scenery, lights, etc., of their play, will be returned. Information is best given, and asked for, by means of a comprehensive questionnaire; this should show, when completed, the names and addresses of the society, its secretary, producer, and S.M. with 'phone numbers; the title, setting, and period of the play, the number of its characters, and its net running time; any special requirements, e.g. rostra, backcloths, steps, unusual items of furniture, or effects required by the team to be supplied by the festival authorities; furniture which the team itself will provide. (If the festival is competitive, it would seem fair that the use of properties and furniture supplied by a team should be restricted to that team, and that others should not be allowed to profit by their efforts and enterprise—but this is a matter of policy for the organizers.) Particulars of records to be used must be known, as it is the organizers' responsibility to apply for permission to perform these to the public. (Private recordings are not usually copyright.) Teams should be advised to have their properties identified; tie-on labels showing the name of the society, the play, and date of performance could be used. A warning about fire-proofing should be given, perhaps with particulars of the methods and formulae recommended. Details of the lighting and sound effects (if any) should be clearly provided for, and if the festival S.M. is to be directly responsible for their manipulation, detailed cues must be shown. A final date for the return of the questionnaire and stage-plan should be specified, with a warning that requirements cannot be met with if sufficient and prompt information is not furnished. Some organizers threaten disqualification. In addition, the adjudicator requires a copy of the play. To supply this may be the responsibility of the festival S.M., who will sometimes choose to ask also for a copy for his own scrutiny and use; one copy may serve the double purpose.

All records thus obtained should be carefully filed for reference.

When all the material has been collated, a meeting of producers and S.M.'s should be called, preferably at the venue of the festival, as this will allow the teams to inspect the facilities first-hand. Points and difficulties can then be discussed in detail. As it is unlikely that all teams will be able to use the actual hall for a rehearsal, it may be wise, especially in a competitive festival, to rule this out for all entrants.

During the festival itself the festival S.M. should, if possible, only supervise, and delegate the various jobs to his stage-staff, with the members of which he will have been in close liaison during the previous weeks; but he should be able to take over any back-stage job at short notice (there should be no objection to his and his staff's having their own stage-management rehearsal at the hall). Clear notices should show the competing societies the dressing-rooms allocated to them, but the conduct and preparedness of the members themselves is the responsibility of the society's own S.M. Also a responsible member of the team (producer or S.M.) should report to the festival S.M. on arrival. The festival S.M. should make early contact with the adjudicator, who should be accorded the usual courtesies and attention due to a guest. He should be asked if he wishes the final set to be struck (as, properly, it should be) before he takes the stage to give his adjudications; he should also be consulted about the interpretation of the rules, especially those concerned with timing, and he may appreciate being given a choice of position for observing the play; he will certainly *not* appreciate having to work in the dark, and, as trailing flexes are not approved of, he should be supplied with an efficient battery-operated table lamp. About the adjudication itself, he should be asked if he desires the front-of-house lights on or off, and if he wishes to have a table on the stage for his papers, and, perhaps, a chair for demonstration purposes. He may wish to have certain properties, used during the performances, available for similar purposes—or even a "model" to walk the stage; the model is likely to have to be the S.M.

In all festivals, but particularly in those run on competitive lines, the festival S.M. should hold himself at the service of the participants in a co-operative, but impartial, way. The various rules, which are his concern, should also be enforced with equal fairness. Although festivals are voluntary, it should be remembered that people who enter them do so because they take amateur drama seriously, and this may well mean over-sensitive nerves and uncomfortable tension, for which allowances must be made.

CHAPTER IX

TAKING IT FURTHER

The Stage Manager's Material

STAGE management, taken seriously, is an art that gives ample and interesting scope for research and experiment. No opportunity to enlarge the S.M.'s knowledge and experience should be missed. Research will take him into museums, picture galleries, and libraries; he should see as many amateur productions as he can, and look out for new ideas. Most societies will welcome an interested visitor back-stage, provided he is there to learn and to see how others cope with the problems of stage management. The more drama festivals he attends, the better are his own sets likely to be, for he will see not only many different types of setting, but also hear them adjudicated upon by qualified people.

We have said little of the professional theatre, which may suggest many ideas and set high standards, for there is a danger of the amateur striving to imitate a technique and form that ill accord with the amateur theatre. The S.M. will, therefore, take care to study and interpret the technique of professional stage management in terms of the small, moderately-equipped stage, and of the necessarily limited skill and experience of his actors and producer.

We have suggested he should keep his ears open for sounds capable of being represented as stage effects; similarly will he tend to observe everyday things with a calculating eye, for while everything appertaining to drama must be presented in terms larger than life, the final effect must be that of life as it is experienced (except perhaps in the experimental type of play); hence the S.M. should develop an eye for detail. He should carry a note-book with him for noting ideas as they occur—perhaps on a train journey or during a conversation. (For example, the authors were in difficulties over obtaining a large oil-painting of a lady of the nineteenth century. A conversation with a photographer about tinting suggested the idea of colouring a modern photograph with water paints; a valueless photograph was thus made into a useful property.)

As far as books on the subject are concerned the S.M.'s material is inexhaustible. Some books deal specifically—or include chapters on—stagecraft itself. Others, such as those on architecture, English history, ancient history, period furniture, etiquette, etc., will serve for reference purposes.

The *American National Theatre and Academy* (ANTA), 1545 Broadway, New York 36, N. Y., provides an advisory service for professional actors and amateurs. It is an expert body which can help with every aspect of dramatic work whether of an artistic or administrative nature. Other services received by ANTA members include theatre information, placement and job counseling, photographic loan service, and script service. Members also receive the quarterly ANTA *Newsletter*, 10 issues a year of *World Premieres*, and the *National Theatre Service Pamphlets*. Individual membership is $7.50 per year (tax deductible) and anyone interested in the theatre may join this organization which is nationally chartered by Congress. Whether your organization is a little theatre, a youth club, women's institute, townswomen's guild, a church group or a university, college or school dramatic society, you will find the answer to most of your problems through the *American National Theatre and Academy*.

We hope that our reader will always remember that however small his society or drama group, guild, or institute, he (or she) plays a part in a nation-wide activity, the standards of which, though generally as high as they ever have been, still vary enormously. In recent years we have seen, through the television service, amateur performances of which no professional need be ashamed; on the other hand, every week there are dozens of performances throughout the country that merit not merely the description "amateur" (which we hope is losing its suggestion of mediocrity and patronage) but "inescapably amateur"—a term of criticism that all workers in the amateur theatre should fear and fight against.

INDEX (*Production*)

INDEX (*Stagecraft*)